YOU 2 CAN OWN REAL ESTATE

How to Buy, Finance, Renovate, Flip or Hold in Any Economy

Doug McIntyre

10-10-10
Publishing

YOU 2 CAN OWN REAL ESTATE
www.you2canownrealestate.com

First 10-10-10 Publishing Edition 2017

Publisher
10-10-10 Publishing
Markham, ON
Canada

Contents

I dedicate this book to everyone who is mustering up the courage, the know how and funds to invest in real estate, as your home or as an investment. My hat is off to those of you learning, preparing or have taken action to purchase investment property.

I am so very grateful for my Real Estate Teachers along the way. The real estate educators, the tireless realtors in my early days of real estate, and countless investors willing to share their successes and pitfalls with me.

Foreword

I was extremely impressed with Doug McIntyre's understanding of real estate investing, and his depth of knowledge about the real estate industry. His passion for real estate shines through in this entertaining book. He explains clearly how to acquire real estate and be aware of the pitfalls, making this book a must-read if you are thinking about purchasing your family home, or building on your investing portfolio. In You 2 Can Own Real Estate, Doug provides easy to understand information about how to find your perfect home, undervalued property, creative financing, leveraging equity, foreclosures and joint venture projects. The vast amount of information covered in this book highlights the critical skills and knowledge required to build your wealth in real estate.

Whether you are a first time home buyer or a sophisticated investor, this book contains time-tested techniques to build your recession-proof real estate portfolio. Learn to become that savvy investor who can quickly analyze and identify the difference between a great real estate deal and a not-so-good deal. You will learn the investor's secret to staying focused on the prize when times get tough.

I fully endorse this book about claiming your place in the real estate world. Build your family's wealth while earning passive income. You are living in the best time in history to build wealth by owning real estate with focus, determination, and a plan. Remember this is real estate, not rocket science.

Raymond Aaron
New York Times Bestselling Author

Acknowledgements

Thank you to my Family and Friends who are always interested to hear about my latest real estate endeavour.

Educators and investors, Ozzie Jurock and Ralph Case, who run the REAG investing group. Mortgage Brokers, Kyle Green and Dustan Woodhouse, who always make time and clearly explain the media hype. All the Real Estate Action Group members that continually take action and make real estate deals.

Dan Paulson, Tomaz Mirek, Adam Katalski, Tony Hemsley, Shamus Pollock and Hugh the Electrician, for their professional trades work and for making me look so good over the years.

Raymond Aaron, who inspired me to put onto paper my passion for Real Estate.

Cara Witvoet for so enthusiastically guiding and encouraging me through the writing of this book.

Michael Campbell for his business insight on a Macro level, and for his informative weekly radio business show.

Adam and Matt Scalena for their weekly podcast with up to date information and interviews with Real Estate influencers.

How I Got Started

I Have Always Believed in Home Ownership

I was fortunate enough to grow up in a single-detached home and never knew any different. When I moved from home, I shared a house with a couple of friends. While in my early twenties, I was working long hours in construction and was able to save some money.

We were sitting at work one day and a co-worker mentioned he was thinking about selling his house. He was talking about equity, debt servicing, and buying another property. I asked him, "Just how does this mortgage thing work?" I had paid off a couple of small loans by this time and had established a good credit rating. I have to admit that at first, I did not understand how mortgage pay down works, so I asked him to explain a second time how a mortgage works.

It was not long after that I began to work with a Realtor who was recommended to me, and we went hunting. Within a couple of months, I was the owner of my first single-family detached home. I was in shock, thinking "What have I gone and done?" Eventually, the shock subsided, and it was time to move into my *4-bedroom home.* What seemed like the natural decision at the time was to invite my two roommates to come live at my new home. Within a couple of months living in the house I quickly began to understand the benefit of receiving rent each month. I put an ad in the newspaper (this was back in the eighties when Craigslist did not exist) and invited a third person to join us.

Unintentionally, I had created a cash flowing situation. By cash flow I mean the total rent collected was greater than my monthly expenses, putting money in my pocket. We were all friends, so this situation worked very well. We all shared the home doing the things that 20-somethings do. I was like the live-in caretaker, grounds keeper, and occasional peacemaker. My friends were paying rent to me, which in turn paid my mortgage, house expenses, and put some change in my pocket at the end of each month.

I thought to myself, "This is amazing, I could be onto something here!" Granted property prices were lower in the 80's but the concept of rental income versus expenses and having cash flowing has not changed.

How Mortgage Financing Works, and Pay Down

Once your down payment is in place, it gets easier moving forward. When you pay rent, you are paying your landlord's mortgage. Purpose built rental buildings, detached houses, basement suites, and condos are rentable to people, perhaps you, who are unable to put together a down payment for whatever reasons. Monthly rent is paid in exchange for a warm, dry place to call home. When a renter, maybe you, wants a change of scenery or the landlord is a jerk, a month's notice of vacating is given. The renter moves to the next rental suite, will pay a security deposit and, each month, essentially paying down the landlord's mortgage. Paying rent is not a bad thing; I just prefer to receive rent than pay. For you who have the drive and the means to own and invest in real estate, I share my experience in hopes this will help you to seek additional knowledge and resources to make an informed buying decision when opportunity knocks. You are taking the time to read this book so I assume you would like to buy your first or another real estate property.

So, here is a quick education on a mortgage. A monthly mortgage payment is a blend of interest and principle pay down.

Each month, you make a mortgage payment. A portion of your monthly payment is interest and a portion pays down the principle amount borrowed. You pay the lender interest each month for the privilege of borrowing money to purchase your home. But not all your monthly payment is interest. The amount of $ going toward principle is paying down your debt and, in essence, paying yourself. The money paying down your principle contributes to the equity you build in your home. More about equity in a bit.

So, each month instead of paying Joe Landlord, you are paying yourself. The best part of all, you are living in a place you can really call home. Go ahead, paint the walls whatever colour you want without fear of losing your damage deposit.

If you want to buy for investment to rent out now or in the future, then stay tuned; we will go more in depth about this as I go along.

After some time, you may want to take some equity out from your current home and purchase another to rent out. You then become Joe Landlord for someone else to pay down your mortgage.

Sweat Equity For Quick Profit

Sweat equity is another name for paying yourself. Your time and sweat when performing upgrades to a property increases the value, your pay. My name came to the top of the wait list in the Strata Complex where I was living, enabling me to rent my unit. The Bylaw allowed for a maximum of 15% of the total units in our Complex to be rented.

My mortgage had just come up for renewal and I was able to take out some cash, equity that I had built up, for a down payment of another property. So, on my way, I went hunting for a new place to purchase to call home. I had just returned from one of my first trips to Mexico in about 20 years, when I took possession of a bachelor suite in downtown Vancouver. Inspired by my recent trip, I proceeded to paint the walls terracotta orange and yellow; I installed laminate flooring and baseboard moulding, changed a couple of lights, and installed a Murphy bed. No sooner had I finished the upgrades, I heard that the owner of the suite directly across the hall was thinking to sell. I knocked on the door and asked if he would like to sell. He proceeded to show me through the original condition suite, and we negotiated a purchase price on the spot! The important thing to note here is that I had become knowledgeable of pricing in the neighbourhood while searching and purchasing the bachelor suite. Having current knowledge of the real estate market enabled me to negotiate a spontaneous purchase. I cannot stress enough the value of being knowledgeable about the market you are looking at. I later learned that another owner in the building was interested and had attempted to contact this owner to make an offer to purchase. If I was not familiar with pricing, and had needed to go do some homework, the opportunity would probably have been missed.

So again, I had purchased the bachelor suite, using equity pulled out from the unit I was previously living in. I needed to sell the bachelor suite to finance the one-bedroom across the hall. I will add that the spontaneous purchase unit came with an unobstructed view of Downtown and the North Shore Mountains!

I listed the bachelor suite for sale and the first open house netted a sale. The real estate agent told me the purchaser loved the Mexican-inspired terracotta colours.

I had only owned the bachelor suite for a couple months and made money on the sale. Needless to say, this got me thinking. The relatively simple upgrades done to the suite netted me a profit.

Repeat – Learning Along the Way

I continued to buy, renovate, and sell, focusing on rundown units or units in original condition, and in need of updating. After some time, I was tearing out bathrooms and kitchens, and sometimes removing a wall, usually between the kitchen and dining room or altering closet space. Shortly into the first couple of projects, after the demolition, I felt heavy and a numbness come over me when looking at the suite that l had completely gutted and now needed to rebuild. Have you ever thought to yourself, "what have I gone and done?" Like any project, breaking down the work into small increments created a more workable project. I had no grand plan in the beginning, but I had motivation and drive. I am a quick learner when I jump into something with both feet. After a suite is gutted there is no turning back, the only direction is forward.

I have completed projects by hiring a mixture of certified trades-people, or by hiring one tradesperson who hires sub-trades. Some projects had only been myself and a buddy doing most the work, or a mixture of all the above.

I remember one real estate agent telling me that I needed to focus on one type of product. One day I was asking the agent to arrange for me to look at one, then two bedroom condos, and the next day I wanted to look at houses. This was my way of learning what worked best for me, although not recommended. In hindsight, working out my numbers and establishing what I could afford, and the type of product I was looking for, would have saved a lot of time. By the way, I was fired by that Realtor, next.

Over time I developed the savvy to be the deal hunter, purchaser, demolitionist, quasi contractor, designer, and staging decorator. I remember a friend that worked as a decorating consultant telling me years ago not to fear colour when choosing paint. The most inexpensive way to change the feel of any space is paint colour. I will say it is time consuming learning all these skills, but this is just the way I did it. I have since backed off from the hands-on work but am directly involved with the day to day progress of a renovation. Self-managing a renovation is time consuming, but I have more control and stay on top of things by visiting the site daily to see what is going on during construction.

Become Licenced - Continue Forward

As I learned more about the real estate industry, I became more interested in the transactional process of the purchase and sale of property. I put my money down and enrolled in the program to obtain my Real Estate Trading licence. As an investor at heart, attaining my licence complemented the skills and knowledge I had acquired. I worked as a part time agent for 4 years, while still going to my full-time salary job. Eventually, I exited the salary job to pursue full time real estate. I now help home buyers find their dream home, and investors their next revenue property. Real estate is my passion; I feel fortunate to work in a field that I so enjoy. There is endless information and changes in the market to keep up to speed with. Before getting licenced, I always worked with a Realtor when buying or selling property. There are many pieces, and moving parts, when buying and selling real estate and very risking going it alone. Working with a Realtor provides professional service so, if something goes sideways in a transaction, the agent and their Broker will do their best to resolve the situation. Sellers and buyers do take legal action against one another in real estate world, so prior to being a licenced realtor I preferred not be a cowboy and think I knew everything. Buyers and sellers are signing legal documents and to be taken very seriously. Any changes to what is committed to in the contract requires a professional to stick handle the negotiating and ensure a smooth as possible ride to the finish line. I hope you will find some information within this book helpful if you are thinking to purchase your first home or you are on the road to becoming an investor.

The topic of real estate is discussed often in the work place, coffee shops, restaurants, and public gatherings. Because this is my passion I can talk about real estate all day, every day, and I am happy to share some of my experience along this path of property purchasing and investing.

For those of you considering purchasing real estate for your home or for investment purposes, the information here is meant to be a helpful guide, discussing the basics and, hopefully, deepening your drive and desire. Additional research may be required on your part, or you could hire a professional who is competent in their field, whether it be financing, buying, selling, renovating, tax accounts, investment advising, mentoring, or coaching.

Now that I've given you a background on my experience and passion for real estate, it is time to learn how YOU can start earning money with real estate! Head to the next chapter to learn how paying your mortgage each month will make you rich compared to paying rent.

Notes

Notes

Owning Real Estate vs Renting

Do Not Fear Buying Real Estate

You are taking your precious time to read this book so you are thinking can I get into the market? Perhaps you are a home owner and have realized the power of leveraging and you want to create your investing portfolio. You are probably needing to arrange with a bank or mortgage lender a pre-approved amount they will lend you as debt. You will need to show the lender you have a good history of paying down debt and paying your monthly bills. You will need to provide banking history, employment income, and they will check your credit rating. Do not be paralysed by fear with the thought of taking on such a large debt—you are not alone! Millions of hard working people around the developed world enter into agreements to faithfully pay a prearranged amount of money each month to their financial institution.

Discussing the real estate market is a common topic of late, often driven by people's perceived inability to enter the market: the market is going up; I'm too late to get in; the market is slowing; mortgage qualifications change; market is on a tear and going up again; the bubble is going to burst; household debt is at record levels. The reality is that real estate generally goes up; the media enjoys creating sensational headlines with respect to the real estate market. I have seen headlines recycled but then, when I read the article, it has very little to do with the headline. We are all busy and often only read the headlines producing a rollercoaster of emotions. Headlines are often created with outdated information, or produced as an opinion piece. Everyone has an opinion on everything. If you want to sell your news are you going to print headlines that grab the reader's emotion or some boring headline saying the real estate market is doing well, go out and have a nice day. Sure, there are precautions we need to take when making a large purchase. Make an educated decision using up to date and relevant information.

Look at history and the overall rise in real estate

values; there is a pattern—up! Granted, markets are often in flux but, when viewed on a graph (www.you2canownrealestate.com), you will see micro rises and drops over the years. Take the long view; see how the values, over time, have risen a tremendous amount!

The lending institution you choose will review your financial situation and lend you an amount that fits into your debt servicing ability. Mortgage lenders use a formula adding your total monthly debt put against your total monthly earnings with a required amount of your earnings remaining. The banks and mortgage lenders have an interest to ensure that you, the home owner, is not put into an over extended situation and unable to fulfill the lending agreement—basically, unable to make the monthly payments. Your bank or lender much prefers to have you live happily in your home, paying manageable monthly mortgage payments. The lender takes no pleasure in placing a property into foreclosure, legally forcing the owner out and reselling the property on the open market. Costs add up quickly for a bank to hire a property management company to secure the property, make any repairs, paint and sell on the open market. Lenders are in the business of lending money, not foreclosing and reselling property. This is time-consuming—costing a lender money. Okay, so let's say you have put together a down payment. Your monthly mortgage payments are often around the same amount as the rent you are paying. This is the glorious part of home ownership; once in your home, the payments are often around the same as when you were renting! For the newer investor, you might be asking how exactly you can use the equity in your home to purchase more real estate. Excellent question! Perhaps you have budgeted, working hard saving, or you have come into some money and want to add to your real estate portfolio. If you have equity in your home, there are a variety of ways you can leverage equity to use toward a down payment to purchase more properties. "So you say, but then I'll be paying two mortgages versus paying my one." Double the payment, double the responsibility you say. Stay with me here because it gets better, not more stressful. Real Estate debt is what I call good debt. Having debt on a boat or recreational toys, although very fun, would be considered not so good debt. Those toys depreciate over time versus real estate increases in value over time. We all enjoy our toys and I sure have my own. I am wanting to illustrate the difference in debt that works for you and debt you have for your amusement and entertainment. If you want your money to work for you, continue reading. More is going to be revealed.

As markets rise, you increase your net worth by way of appreciation on the value of your properties. Let's use the stock market as an example, or an investment fund for that matter, here it is: If you earn 7% annual interest on a $100,000 investment, you would earn $7000. Not a bad return but this is where it really gets exciting! If you put the $100,000 as your down payment (20%) to purchase a $500,000 home when the market goes up 7%, you have earned $35,000 in equity. You earn 7% on the $500,000 versus earning 7% only on the $100,000 you initially contributed. As an example, refer to the graph, illustrating over time, earnings from the stock market vs real estate (www.you2can ownrealestate.com). With real estate, you are earning money on the entire value of your property. If you have multiple properties, add the market value together of all properties; then, multiply the percentage (%) the market has risen, and this will tell you how much equity your properties have risen and also represents the increase in your net worth! Stay tuned on this one.

Pay Yourself Every Month vs Your Landlord

Obviously, we are all familiar with the concept, when you rent, you give a pre-determined sum of money on the 1st of each month to the landlord so you can stay for another month. When you decide to leave, you clean the place, maybe have deducted the cost from your security deposit to pay for a small repair and, then, receive the remainder of your security deposit. The cycle begins again: pay your security deposit, sign a one-year lease, and pay monthly an agreed upon amount to your landlord. All the money paid as rent is gone, never to be seen again.

You work hard, day after day, prioritizing where and what to spend money on. Maybe you put money into RRSPs or RESP, or the stock market, work sponsored pension, or a TFSA to create a nest egg of savings for those later years commonly referred to as retirement. These are all worthy and safe investing vehicles for parking money and earning a modest amount from.

Every mortgage payment you make at current interest rates, at the time of writing this book, half your monthly payment goes to interest and half goes to pay down the principle amount owing on the mortgage. When you are paying down the principle, this amount of the monthly payment is paying yourself. This is reducing the amount owed to the lending institution and, therefore, you keep more of your money. As mentioned earlier, as property appreciates, this is a windfall for owners. You pay yourself each month by paying down the principle owed to the bank, and over time you increase your equity. Basic math on equity is: the present market value of your home minus the amount owing to the bank = equity. The monthly amount paid to your mortgage, with today's historically low interest rates, equals the amount you would pay as rent. The huge difference when owning your property, you are steadily increasing your equity every month and also receiving the benefit of your property value rising over time. Using historical interest rate of say 5-7% with a new mortgage, in the early years more of your monthly payment goes toward interest and less paying down your mortgage loan (principle). Over the years, steadily paying down your mortgage debt until, eventually most of your monthly payment goes toward paying down your mortgage loan (principle) and a lesser amount goes to pay interest.

Yes, markets fluctuate and corrections occur but, over time, property owners are in a win-win position. After 25 years, or sooner, you make a whole lot of "dough, moolah, shekels, wampum, clams, scratch"—in your home! The renter has nothing for paying month after month, year after year, but you found the courage, scrapped up a down payment, made your monthly payments and paid off your mortgage. Now that is a nest egg! It's another great example, when owning real estate, outside forces drive property values higher and higher.

Property Appreciation and Mortgage Pay Down

Bear with me for this math portion. The importance of understanding how mortgage pay down and appreciation works is so very important. The traditional method of purchasing property goes like this: a minimum down payment of 10% for personal residence is required to obtain a mortgage. CMHC – Canadian Mortgage and Housing Corporation gets involved when less than 20% is applied to a home purchase. Basically, if you have 10% down, CMHC funds and insures an additional 10% to total 20% down for your purchase. Banks only loan up to 80% of the value of a property, commonly referred to as LTV (loan to value). The rules have changed recently, so best you speak with a local Realtor or Mortgage Broker to obtain up to date information.

On a side note when a mortgage holder does not make their mortgage payments the property can be put into foreclosure. Most people have heard about someone who got a great deal on a foreclosure. There can be large discounts when purchasing a foreclosed property from the bank. I will go into more detail about foreclosures in an upcoming chapter.

Okay, so let's say, Joe and Jan put a 10% deposit of $50,000 toward the purchase of a $500,000 home. Using an appreciation value of 3% each year, at the end of 5 years, Joe and Jan's property will be worth slightly more than $575,000—an increase of $75,000 just on the appreciation! Stay with me now, using a simple calculation after 5 years of mortgage payments, they will have paid down $65,000 of their debt to the bank. So, the property value increased 75K + debt pay down of 65K = Joe and Jan being $140,000 richer than they were 5 years ago.

Joe and Jan's original commitment was a down payment of $50,000. After 5 years, the market appreciation returned an additional $75,000. This is the power of leverage! That is phenomenal return on their money! This is truly the incredible returns people receive from real estate as an investment. Using an annual market rise of 3% a year, Joe and Jan earn $15,000 a year, over and above the original value of their home. I am using conservative numbers with this example. It is not costing Joe and Jan anything to live in their home because the appreciation cancels the interest they pay to the bank each month.   If Joe and Jan were to receive 3% interest from $50,000 invested in a mutual fund, they would make approximately $7,500 after being invested for 5 years. So let's do the math, $75,000 - $7,500 = $67,500 difference over the 5 years! "Yeah, but, you say...?" Okay, let's use a very generous 10% interest for a traditional investment vehicle. Joe and Jan invest $50,000, after 5 years they would earn approximately $25,000—a difference in earning of $50,000 in favour of real estate. Jan and Joe are earning from the entire value of their property, increased equity and making money from borrowed money, their mortgage. Now that is leverage! Using numbers from above, 50K (appreciation) + 65K (mortgage pay down) = 115K. Any way you slice it leveraging from real estate over time almost always beats traditional investing. A very savvy investor makes very good returns from the stock market. The average person is not a savvy stock investor.

So, you can see the property appreciation + mortgage pay down puts any homeowner so much farther ahead financially, versus renting. For the investor, multiply this by 2, 3, or maybe 4 properties. This is a mind- blowing return on your money!

Largest Ever Unreported Inflation

I will spare you the in-depth explanation of how inflation works. It is important to understand that as inflation continues to rise, so will real estate values.

Inflation can be described as the cost of a collection of goods and services considered to be the necessities for daily living, is calculated on a monthly frequency. One could challenge the accuracy of the inflation rate quoted in recent times because some products we consume daily have been removed from the overall calculation. Products that were once in the inflation calculation, and commonly referred to as CPI, (Consumer Price Index), have since been removed as the cost of the product or service escalated and would dramatically increase the stated inflation rate. Another way to describe inflation; as prices increase, more dollars are required to purchase the same item, therefore more dollars are required to purchase the same piece of real estate. This is a conversation for another day. I encourage you to read some online material to better understand inflation. It took me a while to clearly understand how inflation works and its effects on purchasing power. As one of my mentors has said, "We are living in a time with the greatest unreported inflation rate."

Let's say the cost of a product you purchased last month cost $100, then this month the same product cost $102, you just experienced a month to month 2% increase with inflation and you are left with less money in your pocket at the end of the day. Don't fret my rising real estate stars; property values increase along with inflation. As inflation rises, so does the value of hard assets. Real estate, being a hard asset, rises alongside inflation.

When city populations are increasing, this causes a limited supply of product, forcing the price to increase—basic business 101 concept here of supply and demand. When there is more demand, this causes less supply and cost rises. Some cities are challenged with limited land to build real estate projects. City planners and private developers experience development and economic constraints that generally limit the speed of development. Some will say that cities control the speed and quantity of development. Cities have their duty to consult with neighbourhoods, hold public meetings and direct development toward an overall future plan. Developers stay focused with the health of the economy, economic cycles, and purchasing trends. They do not necessarily want to build as much as possible, with the real possibility that they could get stuck holding a whole lot of inventory of unsold condos and no buyers.

Another piece of the inflation equation is that when additional money is printed by government then people have more money to spend on the same number of goods. People are then willing to spend more money on hard assets like real estate therefore increasing the value. I am not an economist and not meaning to confuse the topic at hand here being real estate. I just want to encourage you to gather more information to better understand the forces behind currency value and how it effects real estate.

Cash Flow Property in a Calm or Turbulent Market

Maybe you are thinking of purchasing a house with a suite that you can rent out as an income generator, also known as a mortgage helper, to supplement your mortgage payment, great!

Perhaps you are ready to purchase or you might be a few years from being the investor or aspiring investor that purchases that single-family house, duplex, 4-plex, or condo unit. When purchasing for investment, leave your emotions out of the purchase decision. Purchasing a home for you and your family takes into consideration proximity to schools, room for your family to grow, entertain and where you feel good. Purchasing for investment has different considerations, the income versus expense numbers, location, and integrity of structures are important criteria and your guiding light. Lot size or possible rezoning could also be considerations if you would like to redevelop the property in the future. It is very important to work out your numbers before going shopping, so that when you come across a possible purchase, you can take quick action and present an offer. A less stressful investment will put money in your pocket every month or worst case scenario you break even after all expenses are subtracted from the rent you collect. Each and every payment you make to the bank or lender a portion goes to pay interest on borrowed money and a portion goes toward increasing your equity. Each month, you are paying down your debt to the bank and increasing your net worth!

For example, you purchase a house with one suite on the main level and one suite in the basement or a duplex. You collect two rent checks every month. Your expenses would be: the mortgage payment; annual house insurance; annual city utilities, annual property tax; repair/maintenance fund; property management fees, if applicable; any additional local government billing; and strata or operating fees, if buying into a multi-family complex. Add your costs for the year, divide by 12 months to arrive at a monthly cost. Subtract your monthly expense from the rent you collect, and you have either a surplus or a deficit. Hopefully, you have surplus, some money left over after paying all the bills. I speak often about cash flow but if all your expenses are covered by your rental income then you are okay. Over time, expenses increase, as will the rent you charge. Just nice to have a buffer with cash flow at the end of the month.

So best case scenario, you are paying the investment property bills from the rent proceeds. You will sleep at night with a smile on your face knowing you are paying down your mortgage, appreciating property value, and putting some money in your pocket at the end of the month.

Another quite important part of investing to mention is when you have a cash flowing property, you are immune to a fluctuating real estate market. Rent is collected each month, mortgage paid, all bills paid, and some green in your pocket. The market can do whatever it does while you continue to lower your debt and increase your net worth. You might choose to use the cash flow to further pay down your loan to pay down your mortgage quicker. If and when the market experiences a correction or a slow period, you continue paying down your mortgage each month and put some green in your pocket. Your monthly costs do not change with market fluctuation, all your expenses continue to be covered by the rental income. If the market was to enter a correction period, history shows the market will recover, and you resume increasing your net worth through the rising value of your property. Something to note: as your mortgage amount steadily decreases, your cash flow increases! Over time less of your mortgage payment goes toward interest and more goes to pay down your debt. Eventually, your investment property is paid off; the money, which in the past went toward the mortgage, is now all in your pocket, 100% cash flow! This will make a huge lifestyle change when it is time to retire or you want to decrease the number of days of work per week.

If you are not already a property owner are you getting a better understanding the financial advantages to owning your home, or investment property versus renting? The financial rewards are staggering when you compare paying down your mortgage and, therefore, increasing your net worth—versus thousands of dollars gone forever, paid out in rent. If you are not completely clear on this concept keep reading. Once you are set up with a property time is your friend.

I wish for all of you that this concept of paying yourself each month WILL become reality and make you rich! Keep reading, and I will tell you about the people who are going to help you find the cash flowing and money investment properties.

Notes

Notes

Notes

Choosing Your Professional Team and Financing Your Purchase

Why Have Professionals on Your Team?

In my younger years, I thought I knew a lot about many things. Life has taught me different. Perhaps better but I know today it is okay to ask for help and not try to do everything myself. Today, with Realtor.ca, Craigslist, and Kijiji, the average person can gather much more information compared to a short time ago. A Realtor who has listed a property for sale would be happy to deal with a buyer who has no professional representation. The prospect buyer could arrange their own inspection, go to a bank and secure a mortgage, and close the deal. Do you really want to make one of the largest purchases of your life, relying on your own limited experience? Many people are quite knowledgeable about a lot of things, but the average person, including myself, cannot possibly know every detail as it relates to a real estate sale or purchase. The services of professionals could save you heartache and perhaps thousands of dollars. A savvy, independent mortgage broker can save you thousands of dollars during the term of your mortgage. A motivated and experienced real estate agent will work with you until you find the home or investment property you are looking for. A caveat here is that buyers and seller's expectations at times do not match the current market conditions. A seller's good memories experienced in their home has no value to a buyer. A buyer can have a long or tasteful wish list for what they want in their home but their budget does not permit. A professional will educate and guide the client through the processes.

A qualified home inspector will identify possible problems or, at the very least, bring to your attention any repairs that may arise in the future; some money can be put aside or saved for a future expense. Deficiencies in a home inspection can be used to negotiate a lower purchase price. There are no shortage of sad stories; purchaser of a house chooses to waive the opportunity for an inspection, only later to find out the foundation leaks water into the basement, or an unauthorized renovation was done in the house.

These types of repairs spell money—lots of it!

When spending such a large amount on a home, trying to save a few hundred dollars on an inspection or having professional representation can cost so much more over time. Professionals have a legal obligation to serve their clients and will go to bat for a client if any legal issues arise.

Thousands of real estate transactions occur every day in North America. The majority of transactions go through without a problem. Many transactions do not flow in a straight line from the time a prospect buyer writes a contract to purchase to the time of possession. A myriad of things can happen before possession date so a lone wolf navigating the wild with lawyers and banking professionals can get eaten up. There is always a possibility of a deal going sideways and, if you are on your own, the legal bill will be staggering. One example is a water pipe bursts in a unit directly above yours 3 days before you are to move in. You cannot stay in your present location because the new owners take possession in 3 days. Your new condo is not inhabitable because of extensive water damage, what do you do? Who is liable? Where do you live? Where do you put your household belongings? Do not go alone.

Meet Your Professional Team

Mortgage Broker, Realtor, Home Inspector, Lawyer or Notary, and maybe a Financial Advisor are professionals to have on your team.

If someone you trust recommends a professional because of their positive experience I suggest you seriously inquire about the service they offer and arrange your own personal interview. A positive referral from someone you trust is gold.

Most mortgages are secured through a bank, Credit Union, or mortgage company, commonly referred to as secondary lender. One other source of mortgage money is the private lender. Private lending is typically used by the more seasoned investor. A private money loan is often for a short term at a higher rate of interest than the bank, plus an administration fee charged up front. This type of buyer may not be able to satisfy the requirements of a traditional lending institution. The lender secures the loan more based on the value of the property versus the borrowers banking and credit history. If the loan goes bad the lender is legally entitled to the property.

In general, the bank offers to loan money on a *one size fits all* sort of criteria. Generally speaking they offer a set term mortgage with a locked in or variable interest rate. I now introduce to you possibly your next best friend, the independent mortgage broker. He or she is an independent broker, working under the umbrella of a mortgage company. They typically work from home and have access to money from numerous lenders, often providing a more favourable interest rate. More will be discussed about the mortgage broker in the next section.

When you call a real estate agent, you are not automatically committed to working with him or her. I encourage you to interview Realtors and work with one that either has been recommended by someone you trust or one that you feel comfortable with. You need to be comfortable and have good communication when shopping for your home or investment property. If you are buying real estate for an investment, work with an agent that is investor friendly. By this I mean an agent that works with investors and has a keen eye for a deal or willing to put in the time often required to find a good investment property. There are additional considerations when looking for an income generating property versus your home. Investment property searching requires the agent to be sharp with the numbers. You might also take into consideration future zoning for multi-family development that would play out very profitable for an investor. Basically, most favourable locations for a rental property are near transit, schools, businesses and amenities, as in banks, shopping and restaurants. For the patient investor have the Realtor call you when he comes across a deal that fits the type of investment you are looking for.

As mentioned earlier, a qualified home inspector is worth every dollar he or she charges. I'm presuming you would be excited with the prospect of a new purchase; I know I usually am. Unfortunately, excitement, dreamy thoughts of a new home and emotion can be blinding. An inspector will provide you with a detailed report while conducting a thorough inspection of the subject property. The report will outline structural details, as well as major systems and components, providing you with a better understanding of the property. Any defects or problems can be dealt with by the seller as a condition of sale or negotiate a lower purchase price relative to the cost of repairs.

A lawyer or notary are required to transfer title from the seller to you. A Notary Republic is slightly less expensive compared with a lawyer. They both check there are no liens against the property to ensure a clean title to move forward with the transfer of ownership. They take care of all the legal details that the average person struggle to understand. When all is in order they give instruction to the bank or lender to move ahead to move funds. There are many details and timing is of the essence with the work the lawyer does. This is not my area of expertise so I will not go into great detail. Lawyers and Notaries go to school for many years and I would be a fool to think I could tell you exactly what they do. Most important for you to know is that they will ensure the legal documents are in order with your purchase, or sale. Some differences exist in regard to transfer of title; I encourage you to seek more information about this.

Bank, Mortgage Company, or Private Money Lender

One of the first things you need to do before you go property shopping is to get qualified by a bank or independent broker. The qualifying I refer to here is knowing how much money the bank will loan you to buy your home. This information is important so you can set the price range of homes to view. There is nothing more frustrating, and a waste of everyone's time, than to present an offer to purchase a home, only to find out you cannot borrow enough to purchase it! Or worse you have entered into a legal binding contract to purchase a property only to find out you cannot borrow enough money to pay the seller. Can you imagine the emotional stress? Life has its share of challenges, do not create more for yourself by going blindly into a deal. Think about this, you had been searching for weeks, perhaps months, and you find a home that has everything on your wish list. You and your significant other are excited about a property you have made a conditional agreement to purchase. You go to the bank or mortgage broker, provide the necessary financial information for your purchase, and then wait for approval. The excitement is overwhelming. Days pass and you are thinking about how to decorate, your kids have chosen their bedrooms, what route you will drive to work, and the housewarming party you will have. Oops, you do not qualify to borrow the amount needed to purchase the home. Don't create disappointment for yourself. The first thing you want to do is get qualified so you are armed and ready to go hunting!

My experience has been that, more times than not, an independent mortgage broker will get the better mortgage overall compared to the bank. The mortgage broker deals with multiple lenders and is able to deal with a lender that is most friendly to your financial situation. A broker can shop around, sort of speaking, and find a lender that fits your financial situation whereas the bank offers their own line of mortgage products, and you need to fit into their requirements.

An independent broker is self-employed, paid a commission from each mortgage they arrange. The broker is paid when business is completed. The broker has a vested interest to work hard for you in hopes that you will tell your friends and family about the fantastic service you received. The Broker can often get you a lower interest rate mortgage that will save you thousands of dollars during the time of your loan. The broker has an interest to get you the best mortgage possible in hopes that you will contact him or her the next time you're in the market for a mortgage and that you tell your family and friends about them.

Some banks offer competitive interest rates and terms of repayment, compared with an independent broker. Always read the small print! There are usually a select number of banks that do consistently offer an attractive interest rate. Banks will offer a special rate occasionally so timing can work in your favour. If you have the time, shop around and get familiar with the different mortgage products available. If you have a good relationship with the bank, and you are comfortable dealing with the bank, then the bank is a good option for you. Not that long ago I secured a limited time, special rate variable interest mortgage half a percent below their competitors. One year later I received a letter telling me the interest rate was increasing half percent because the banks costs have risen. Huh? I made an appointment with one of the managers and he told me during our meeting that the bank will not be reviewing my rate increase. Beware and read the fine print!

What mortgage term length is best for you? Do you lock in your interest rate or go for a variable rate? Do you want to make payments monthly, every 2 weeks, or weekly? What amortization length is best for you? Your bank or independent mortgage broker will navigate you through this area of the lending process. There are economic factors you need to take into consideration when choosing the type of mortgage that is best for you. A third type of lender is the private money lender. A fee is paid upfront to do business, and the interest rate is higher compared to a standard mortgage lender. There are times when a good or non-traditional deal will come along and the purchaser requires private money because a traditional lending institution would not fund the purchase. The money is often needed for only a short duration of time, or sometimes investors or a small business get stretched financially and require the need for private cash. Sometimes the timing of a deal does not match with the timing when the investor has funds available. Perhaps a business person will receive funds from the sale of their property in one month. They need funds now to secure the purchase of this new opportunity, private money! This is typically for the more seasoned business person or investor.

What is Your Long-Term Investing Plan?

In a perfect world, you would follow through with everything you intended to do. You would say everything you wanted to say to those you love. You would only eat healthy foods, get all the sleep you require to feel rested and exercise regularly to maintain the weight that makes you happy. Few of us do everything that is good for us but we can certainly influence our future.

Establishing a long range financial plan to buy real estate will create the results you desire. Because you are reading this book, you have the desire to own your home or, perhaps, a revenue property, or multiple revenue properties. There are numerous studies that show those of you who make a plan, set goals, and commit it to paper and review often, are far more probable to attain your goals compared to others who wish, dream, or think they could never attain what they desire. Your life is probably busy and you are constantly dividing your time between all the demands of family life, work, clubs, sports, health, school, etc. My purpose here is to, hopefully, educate you a little and create a desire to learn more about real estate. This is not a goal setting book, but investing requires confidence in yourself, your informed decision making and the patients of long term planning.

How you want your real estate portfolio to look influences how you invest. If you want a nice home for your family, work hard and pay that off—great! You may want to lock in your mortgage interest rate for a 5-year term so your monthly payment (would) will not change for the duration of the 5 years. By having a locked in term, you can budget your family expenses so that you have enough for each monthly payment. There are many uncertainties and financial needs with raising a family, so having your mortgage payment the same each month is peace of mind.

For the investor, you may not want to drop all your cash into one property but rather keep some money back for the next property to buy. The interest paid on revenue property or business mortgages is an expense to be claimed against your income at tax time. How many properties do you want to acquire? Maybe you want to live in a house with a secondary suite in the basement. Maybe you are going to eventually rent out your current home and purchase another to live in. Maybe you want one additional cash flowing property that your tenant will eventually pay off. That strategy would net you decent monthly income in later years. Maybe you want to purchase an "old timer" house to live in while you obtain city permitting and build a new home.

The idea I am stressing is to have some idea of what you want to attain in your portfolio. You would not leave your home wanting to go to the store and just start walking down streets hoping to come across a store. When you leave your home you have a plan, I am going to visit this and that store to successfully make the purchase of whatever it is you want. Your long-range plans will influence your purchase today and how you structure financing. Plans can be changed, life changes along with our long-range plans. Do not fear the plan, it is your plan.

Is Working with a Realtor Really Necessary?

"Those Realtors make so much commission. What do they do for their money? I could do that. Why do I need a Realtor anyway?" These are comments and the attitude of many. These were some of my own thinking before becoming licenced.

Obviously, I cannot help but be a little biased here because I am now a licenced Realtor. Before obtaining my licence, I always hired the services of a Realtor. There are so many moving parts to a real estate transaction. I knew that I could not competently know everything there was to know about buying and selling real estate. With selling a property, the MLS system has the largest exposure to buyers than any other online system. There is a ton of due diligence that is done before making a purchase or signing that contract, agreeing to a sale. If any part of a deal goes sideways, you have the expertise and knowledge of the real estate industry behind you. If you are a lone wolf, acting on your own, well, you are on your own, along with your high paid lawyer. Perhaps you are more savvy or well-seasoned, and you are willing to take a risk to act on your own, or with limited assistance from an agent— great.

I always liked the idea of my property, when listed with an agent, having full exposure on the MLS (Multi Listing Service). Thousands of agents across the region and abroad have access to view the listing. If I was to act alone, I could post my property on Craigslist or Kijiji. What would I need to do to host an open house? How would I get the exposure to tell people who are looking to buy that I was having an open house? How would I negotiate a price? How would I fill out the sale contract, which is a legal binding document? How do I know the real value of my property? What if

I have some glitch with financing and I will require more time before taking possession? The nightmare scenarios are plenty and wide scope, believe me. A seller can pay a fee to have their property posted on the MLS and the owner manages everything from there. This method rarely produces optimum results.

For all the reasons above, I recommend hiring the services of an agent who comes recommended, or who you feel comfortable with and have good communication.

Remember, the agent works for you. You always have the final say.

Now that I have outlined the professional people available to help, do not make excuses, taking action.

Read on, and I will further prepare you to take action and be active in the exciting world of real estate! The best is yet to come.

Notes

Notes

Notes

Real Estate for Your Home vs Investment

Your Home – Your Sanctuary

You are pre-qualified for a mortgage, it's time to go shopping—woohoo!

Let's for a moment look 6 months or a few years into the future. It's the end of the day, you come home, take off your shoes, hug the kids, kiss your wife or husband, and look around, and you are proud knowing this is your castle and your sanctuary. Perhaps you are younger and, or single, and you prefer to be in the entertainment district and where the action is.

There are considerations when choosing real estate for your home opposed to buying solely for investment purposes. Your home is where you want to feel good when you are there. Your family will grow up and you will create life long memories. Your decision is based on price and on location: schools, transit, work, amenities, and green space, in proximity to your home. You need to live somewhere; the debt on your home will decrease every month with each mortgage payment you make. Every month, your net worth increases through the pay down of your mortgage and gradual appreciation of your property. Do not fear debt.

So, when shopping for your home, be mindful that you are going to spend a lot of time there. You work hard; find yourself a home that is affordable and that you look forward coming home to.

You may have heard the term *they are working for their home* versus *living in their home.* Some people take on too much debt—maybe through doing renovations on their home or by purchasing the absolute, highest priced home they could afford. Surprise expenses are a way of life; car repairs, medical, home repairs etc. Home ownership quickly becomes a burden when you have no money left at the end of the month for entertainment or to purchase some of the things you enjoy. If your home becomes a financial burden, you will not be a happy camper. I have known people who were drowning in debt and had to sell. Once you are out of the market, it can be tough to get back in. You could be saving for a down payment and chasing the market as it rises. As the market rises, so does the amount required for a down payment. Even if you are to downsize, fees will eat up a chunk of your down payment. What often will happen is by the time the financial burden is gone stress has worn you down. Better to be slightly cautious when buying, so you have some jingle in your pocket to pay for those extra things you enjoy.

Home ownership will get old really quick if you get an uncomfortable feeling or a knot in your gut because you are drowning in debt. Time is on your side when invested in real estate. Be patient; purchase within your budget and your investment will grow.

Corrections Happen – Real Estate Goes Up Over Time

Daily headlines in the media make my head spin: Market is on a rampage; sales are slumping this month; the bubble is going to burst; prices are out of reach; affordability is eroding; interest rates are on the rise; etc., etc. The headlines are endless, and there is always some truth to a headline, but media is in the business of selling their product. The up to date or entire story is often omitted in articles I read online and in print. If a headline stirs your emotions, it is more probable you will continue reading. The media has an important role—investigating and reporting news. The reports on real estate just get blown out of context and are often confusing. Media often focus on the short term or a past time. I read articles about real estate that are out of date. Stories about yesterday's market or some small item that grabs your emotions but not relevant today. Markets are changing and in flux a lot of the time, sometimes in a prolonged slump, but in time values go up.

I know people who have been waiting for the past 15 years for prices to drop. Real estate values have no less than doubled in major cities of Canada, and some regions have tripled in the past 15 years. Those people are still sitting on the sidelines, renting. Many of those people will never purchase real estate in their lifetime. Fear, lack of knowledge, misinformation, stubbornness—who knows for sure what motivates people to continue renting? Single parenting, family obligations or physical challenges can be a barrier to home ownership. We all do what we can to provide for family members and live within our limitations so I do not look down on anyone who is a tenant. This book is about home ownership so this is my focus here.

Landlords need tenants, so renters are your friends. As a landlord you have an obligation to provide clean and safe living space, so your rental suite should receive attention and any repairs when required done immediately. Always in your best interest to keep a good tenant happy.

Real estate values do not go up in a straight line. The market may be on fire for a while and go up 6–15%, then cools off and goes down 2–5%. History of real estate values on a graph shows a jagged line that overall has risen over time (www.you2canownrealestate.com).

Do not be concerned where the market is in a cycle, you are always paying down your debt to the bank and increasing your net worth. If you are cash flowing a revenue property, then you are immune to market fluctuations. Your renter is paying down your mortgage, all your expenses are covered, and you are putting some green in your pocket. For the investor, cash flow is King! Worst case scenario you break even at the end of the month. When the market rises, the increase in property value is a bonus. You are paying down your mortgage each month, and you are also benefitting from property value increasing. I know I repeat many times in this book of cash flow, mortgage pay down and appreciation. These three conditions pay you a very handsome return of your original down payment on real estate.

Real estate can make you money in a short time in a rapidly rising market but, generally, it is a long, simmering type of investment. Go into your investment with the mindset for the long haul. If your situation or investing goals change along the way, sell, take your profit and move on. Do not allow sensational headlines and hyped up conversation to shake your confidence in real estate. Speak with successful investors. Talk with property owners; ask them if they would have done it any different if they had the opportunity to do it over again. I bet you would have difficulty finding anyone who regrets purchasing real estate.

Rental Property – Location and Cash Flow

Location, and cash flow, is king! If you live in a moderate to large size city, try to locate your property search close to transit, shopping, amenities, a large employer, hospital, or post-secondary institution. For example, a hospital employs hundreds of people. There is a steady demand for rental stock in that area for a long time.

Near, or on a major transit line, will be a more desirable location for tenants versus having to walk further than 500 meters to catch a bus or train. Amenities like a bank, grocery store, department store, dry cleaners, and fast food restaurants are amenities that attract a renter to your property. The more convenient your location is to these amenities the more people apply to rent your property, giving you a better selection who you choose as a tenant.

Offering a rental suite away from amenities decreases your rental pool and also decrease the amount you can charge for rent. Ideally you want to have a few prospects to interview so that you can choose the best candidate. Offering a rental out of the way or near an industrial area reduces the number and quality of candidates. Certain people that engage in certain activities prefer to be in undesirable and out of way areas. Choose your tenant wisely. It is very dangerous to have to accept the lone applicant because you do not want to miss another month with no income to pay your mortgage.

A couple of important characteristics of an investor is a blend of persistence patients when looking for an investment property to purchase. When you find a good property, but the numbers do not work and the rental income does not cover all the monthly expenses, just say, "Oh well, next." A good investment does not require you to subsidize every month to pay the bills. Some markets are more difficult to cash flow unless you have put a substantial down payment when purchasing. Putting down a larger than 20% down payment is okay for those investors with deeper pockets. This strategy works in markets where the property values are rising and, therefore, increasing equity in the property. The investor can then sell and receive the difference in cash value from time of purchase to time of sale. This type of speculative investing is riskier but can be quite lucrative for the savvier investor. A more seasoned and knowledgeable investor is better suited for speculating.

For the average investor, as mentioned earlier, receiving some income every month after all your expenses are paid, cash flow, you have yourself a great investment.

Look Within – Do You Really Want to be a Landlord?

You have been working hard, have saved up enough money, or are using some equity from your home as a down payment on an additional property. You are clearly eager to learn more because you are still reading this book. Not to discourage you from buying investment real estate, but being a landlord is not for everyone. Some years ago, before being licensed, I offered to help a friend to interview possible tenants for a rental property. His reply to me was, "I can handle it." He accepted a tenant who paid monthly rent with cash—red flag there—and after a short time, the tenant trashed the apartment and took off.

You need to ask yourself if hiring a property manager would be better to handle your tenant details. What questions do you need to ask to qualify a prospect? How do you check their financial situation, and credit rating? How long have they worked at their job? Do they change jobs frequently? Can you call previous landlords to get a reference? What do you do when neighbours have complained about your tenant's ongoing late night weekend partying?

You do not want to accept a tenant that is borderline because you were unsure how to market your property or you feel uncomfortable to ask the tough questions.

There are techniques to minimize accepting a troublesome tenant. Depending on the region you live in, it can be very difficult to evict a bad tenant once they are in your home.

Are you ready to respond when you receive a call from your tenant informing you the dishwasher is leaking and water has flooded the kitchen? Do you have the expertise to repair plumbing? Do you know who to call outside of business hours?

If managing tenants were easy, everyone would be doing it, right? Completing the due diligence process before accepting a new tenant, to determine whether they are a good tenant or not, will possibly save you a lot of heartache later.

The person I referred to previously, proceeded to accept another tenant that was not so great, and then sold the property after a short time. He quickly became disillusioned with the process of having the tenant pay off his mortgage. It's sad because he was not willing to accept his lack of experience to handle the rental details of his investment.

Creative Financing

Okay, so perhaps you have acquired a couple of properties and you want to increase your portfolio. You have some cash but are unable to carry a mortgage with the bank. Your debt servicing is at the max; Mr. or Mrs. Banker says, "Sorry, investor. We are unable to loan you more money at this time." What now? Do you pay off some of your current mortgage? What you could do is partner up—referred to as a joint venture or JV Deal. You supply the money for the down payment, and your joint venture partner carries the mortgage. You add another property to your portfolio and increase your net worth every month. It is best to draw up legal paperwork with a lawyer when entering in a JV purchase. When dealing with large amounts of money some people seem to lose their moral compass or deviate from the original plan you had discussed when purchasing the property. Believe me this does happen! Legal agreements keep everyone on the up and up.

You find a property that will cash flow, it is a solid structure, and everything looks fantastic, but you have a cash shortfall; you do not have enough for the down payment. You have been qualified by the lender for a mortgage but you need more down payment. You could ask the seller to leave 20% of the selling price in the deal for a specified length of time (say 2 years). A common term for this is vender take-back mortgage. The seller becomes your 20% partner for the first 2 years. Within the 2 years, your property may have gone up in value, in addition to mortgage pay down. At the end of two years, you draw cash out from equity in the property, or from another property, or somehow muster together the 20% to pay the seller. This type of proposal is more attractive to a seller in a flat or inactive market. Often full asking price is offered to the seller and in return the seller leaves the 20% down payment into the deal. A lower than market interest rate can be offered to the seller for the use of the 20%. If a market is rising, the seller could have multiple offers to choose from so not much incentive to keep his 20% value in the deal for 2 years. The vendor take-back agreement works well when the seller's property has been for sale for a while, and he/she wants to be rid of the property and move on but does not want to sell the property at a deep discount. For

2 years, you have been collecting rent and, hopefully having cash flow. The mortgage payments have been reducing your debt every month for 2 years. In addition, going on a conservative appreciation rate of 3% per year for a total of 6% appreciation. With no money in the purchase for the first two years, you have profited the mortgage pay down and the appreciation on the property. You pay the seller back the 20% plus interest. The seller is happy for a full price sale, and interest on the 20% loan for the 2 years.

A line of credit against the equity in your home can make you flush with cash to get into your next real estate purchase. This is called a secured line of credit because you are using the equity in your property as security for the bank. Another mortgage product is part traditional mortgage, and part line of credit secured by equity that you can draw money from. Your broker or real estate agent can explain in more detail about this.

Wow, things are really getting exciting now. In the next chapter, you are going to learn where to find great deals! These are places where investors find great real estate deals!

Notes

Notes

The Buy – Where to Find a Great Deal

What Type of Property Do You Want?

I cannot stress enough the importance to get yourself pre-approved for your mortgage before going shopping, because you know that is where to begin.

Whether you are looking for a single-family house, a house with a mortgage helper suite, or perhaps a strata townhome or condo, you need be clear with yourself so you are not wasting your time nor your Agent's time. Everyone's time is valuable, and we only have so much of it every day. Time management will be covered in my next book— sometime.

Let's say you want a house; you know your budget, and the pricing in the city core is above what the bank will loan you. To find a home in your budget, you will need to adjust your search area outside the city centre or the Suburbs. If you are a city guy or gal, and are not willing to compromise on area, then you will need to alter your wish list. For city living you will need to search for a strata title townhouse or a condo.

If living in a detached, single-family home is non-negotiable, then that is okay. You just need to exercise some flexibility with your search area. Are you willing to compromise and live away from the city centre? If that single-family home is your dream then you will need to search out far enough until the market pricing is within your budget. There is no right or wrong answer here.

If your lifestyle is such that you work and play in the core of the city, then it makes sense to live there. A condo will probably be the better purchase for you. Savings of cash and time can be had by not commuting to work. I personally have friends who work and play in the downtown. They sold their vehicle and signed on with a car share or pay-as-you-go type of set up. Keeping and maintaining a vehicle on the road is not a cheap proposition. If you are a first-time buyer, just getting started, and have limited funds, a pay-as-you-go type of transportation could be a great cost saving alternative for you, and a good alternative for the environment also. I also know of older folks that have ditched their vehicle and joined a car share entity.

The main idea to understand is to get clear with yourself how much, if at all, you will compromise in order to live in your ideal home, whether it be a house, a house with a secondary suite, a condo, or a townhouse. If location is your priority, which for many it is, then you will purchase real estate that fits within your budget.

Where to Search

As an inspiring investor, you may be thinking, "Where do I find the deals?" You have heard the story of Mike's second cousins neighbour, or your co-worker heard about this lady who knew a lady, who got a smoking good deal on a purchase. A couple of obvious places to look is Craigslist and Kijiji, or any other Internet site that has a platform for buy and sell items. FSBO, short for "For Sale By Owner" can net a good deal. Some people just

You 2 Can Own Real Estate

want to handle all the details themselves, not always knowing the true value of their property. Do not fear to negotiate with the seller. It is pretty much expected that any buyer will want to pay less than the asking price. If you offer what is referred to in the industry as a *skunk* or *low-ball* offer, you need to be prepared for any response. The seller may feel disrespected or be surprised by an extraordinary low offer. You have the choice to stay firm with your offer, but be prepared to walk away and think, "Next." You can also raise your offer if you have room to go higher. There can be a lot of emotion tied to a home. The seller may have raised his or her children in the home, hosted family gatherings, celebrated birthdays, did renovations, and is attached to the home.

When searching for the deal you must be diligent and consistent with your search. Often a great deal does not last long before some other deal hunter gets it.

A list of reasons why and the people and places to find deals, and get a lead on a below market property, are as follows: newspapers, neighbours, relatives, banks, FSBO lawn signs, accountants, lawyers, favourite Realtor, any Realtor, obituaries, people divorcing, CMHC foreclosure report, run down houses, MLS expired listings, owner being transferred, fire in house, failing business, people in financial distress, co-workers, inherited property, downsizing, major lawsuit pending, letter to a vacant property, I pay cash for houses ad, mail carrier—and tell everyone you know you are looking to buy property.

You may say, "But approaching someone having financial trouble, or nearing bankruptcy, is unethical." Yes, granted, there are heartbreaking situations where people find themselves drowning in debt. Unfortunately, budgeting and financial planning is not taught in school. Neither you nor I told them to put the trip on their credit card, or to buy the fancy new car. A good used car would have been suffice. Some big spenders create such an enormous debt load for themselves that they are unable to service all their loans. You could be saving them the humility of declaring bankruptcy or defaulting on their mortgage. It is a long humbling road rebuilding a good credit rating. Unfortunately, often big debtors are going to lose their home, whether you buy it or not. A good time to review the fact that building wealth with real estate takes time, so please be patient.

Professional Pillars, Motivated Sellers, Bird Dogs

A number of sources for deals have been mentioned here, but what you want to do is tell EVERYONE you meet, and EVERYONE you know, what you are looking for. Deals often only last a moment. You are not the only person looking and investing in real estate. Do not waste a moment when a deal worthy of purchasing comes along or, at the least, investigate the possible opportunity. Investing can be for the long game but, when you hear of an opportunity, you are like a hot rod, burning jet fuel. You want to become a hungry, no stone left unturned investigator!

You will hear, in investing circles, the term *professional pillars*. The name is referring to professionals who deal with people and are privy to their personal situation. A partial list are lawyers, accountants, doctors, financial advisors, and insurance brokers. You want to speak to these people and let them know who you are and what you are looking for. Follow up with these people periodically to refresh their memory that you are serious and still looking.

Motivated sellers come in all shapes and sizes and often appear without warning. Always be ready to make a deal. When there is a downturn in the real estate market, some inexperienced or impatient investors think the bottom is falling out and they need to sell. This is where media headlines play well for the patient investor. You know that in the long run, values go up. Some buyers jump in because they see their friends investing and they want to make easy money. Unfortunately, these same types of owners do not have the vision or experience to know that property values will recover and eventually rise above the last market peak. This is typically how the real estate cycle works. The exact amount of time it takes for a market to recover is anyone's guess. Refer to the graph (www.you2canownrealestate.com) showing real estate values rise over time.

"What the heck is a bird dog?" you ask. No, it is not a hunting dog or bird retriever. This is the term for a person, or you could call him or her a scout who talks with a lot of people through the course of their day. Maybe the bird dog's work involves crossing paths with other professional pillars. Maybe your bird dog is an accountant who is the first to know when a client's poor financial situation forces them to sell a property. When you are successful in acquiring property through the referral of a bird dog, reward the bird dog.

A finder's fee can be a predetermined amount of cold hard cash, or maybe you write the bird dog into the contract to receive a % of profits when selling if short term deal. A motivated bird dog is worth his or her weight in gold. Someone always knows someone whose brother-in-law's co-worker is needing to sell. Maybe someone your bird dog knows works with someone retiring and moving closer to their children. Maybe a seller is downsizing. Maybe the seller is in a divorce.

If you are accumulating funds to purchase real estate, you can be a bird dog for an investor and receive a finder's fee. What a great no pressure way to talk with people and learn more about real estate. You would learn quickly how people view real estate and this can help you in the very near future.

Foreclosure Court Purchase

We all remember the big economic downturn in the fall of 2008. If you are unsure what that was all about, to explain briefly, mortgages were approved to people who could not afford to pay a mortgage. Initially, they would pay a low rate of interest and, therefore, a low monthly payment. After a pre-set amount of time, say one year or two, the interest rate would reset and increase; hence, substantially increasing the monthly mortgage payments. The mortgages were then bundled into investment vehicles and circulated around the globe. The defaulting on mortgages did not take long to gain momentum as more loans came up for renewal at an increased interest rate. We all felt the pain from that time. I mention this economic downturn period because this produced more properties being foreclosed also here north of the 49th. By Oct 2008 we were all feeling the pain from that time. I mention this economic downturn because this produced a substantial number of mortgages going into default due to non-payment and properties being foreclosed by the bank in the United States and in lower numbers here north of the 49th parallel.

In Canada, the default rate on mortgages is quite low but, although every week of the year, real estate properties are sold in the foreclosure court to the highest bidder. What happens is that a property owner defaults on their mortgage; they stop making payments for whatever reason. Sometimes a marriage breakdown, financial hardship, substance abuse, or mental illness contributes to a property going to foreclosure court. In our region, the bank or mortgage company usually takes possession and secures the property for painting and doing any repairs to make it move in ready and put on the market for sale. The property is listed with a real estate agent, it is advertised on the MLS and showings begin. Eventually, someone will put forth an offer. The lender will quickly review the offer and may respond with a counter offer or accept the original offer. Now, this accepted offer only triggers the property to go to court for final sale. The accepted offer amount is usually public knowledge, although there has been some talk about this changing. Knowing the accepted offer, anyone is welcome to show up on court day, with their realtor, and submit an offer on that same property. The person who submitted the original offer can submit one additional offer higher than the original, knowing that there could be multiple competing offers. The offers, in individually sealed envelopes, are then opened by the judge; the highest offer usually receives the property. When buying a foreclosure, you buy *as is where is.* This method of acquiring real estate works well in a flat market. When a market is active or hot, these properties sell for market value and sometimes above when emotions drive up the bid. I encourage you to speak with your local courthouse and ask when the foreclosure court takes place. Anyone can attend and observe the proceedings.

Joint Venture Partner

Let's say you are the person with the ability to obtain a mortgage and you have some of the down payment. Another eager investor, who might be a tradesperson or handy with tools and has experience renovating, approaches you. This investor has a great deal but only has *some* cash to put toward the down payment. Great! You and your new partner negotiate a joint venture agreement. Your new JV partner contributes some funds toward the down payment; you cover the remainder and secure the mortgage with the bank. Your JV partner is going to do the work on the property in exchange for a percentage of the profit when the property is sold. This arrangement can work well because you are not required to put out any additional cash to pay for the renovations. Carrying costs, including monthly mortgage payments, strata fees, hydro, heating, and renovation costs can make your flip stressful as your available cash diminishes.

You and your new JV partner will want to ensure you have money available for monthly carrying costs and of course renovation costs for material, labour and lastly arrange in writing the split of profits when you get it sold. This JV agreement should be drawn up legally to protect both of you. If the agreement is on paper, neither of you can alter the work and responsibility throughout the project unless renegotiated and agreed. There are endless stories of partnerships going sideways in all business fields because of miscommunication, laziness, greed, and the list goes on. A hand shake is noble but, unless you know your JV partner really well as in your wife or husband, I suggest a legal binding agreement.

Maybe you find a great deal but are not interested to get involved. Maybe you decide to offer the deal to some other investor for remuneration of 5 or 10% of the profit when the property is sold. These agreements are endless with how you can structure them and your contribution to the deal. So, you now have a broad outline where to find deals and sources and the people who can help you find deals. Talk with people to inform them that you are looking for property. You will be surprised how much information will begin flowing back to you when people know you are an investor. In the next chapter, you gain knowledge comparing *freehold non-strata* to *strata* properties. Hold on, because this ride gets better!

Notes

Notes

Notes

What Type of Property and Profit Do You Want?

Freehold or Freehold Strata – What is the Difference?

Common property ownership goes by various names depending on the region in which you live. Here, the most common shared ownership, is referred to as strata title ownership. Some multi-family buildings are lease hold ownership. I will not discuss lease hold here because it is a complete different animal and is not a good investment long term. What Strata title ownership means is you own and are responsible for the unit you live in. You also own collectively and are financially responsible for the maintenance and repair of the common property. Common property is all the space outside the individual units, hallways, parkade, landscaping, pool, exercise areas. I think you get the idea here. What this means is everyone in the complex shares the financial responsibility of funding repairs and general maintenance of the complex— landscaping and cutting of grass, systems maintenance, cleaning and vacuuming hallways, pest control, window cleaning, boilers, elevators. Every owner in the complex is in it together. A board or council is elected by the owners to work with the management company, usually for a one-year term. At the AGM (Annual General Meeting), a new council or board is elected, composed of owners in the complex to steer the operations of the building through the up and coming year. Most of the time a property management company is hired to manage the day to day operations and maintenance of the building. Some complexes are self-managed, but not common.

Freehold property ownership is the detached single-family home, duplex or four-plex. Multi-family, rental building ownership is freehold and beyond the general investing theme that I will discuss for now.

Home ownership was the dream and sign of prosperity in America after the Second World War. Today in many large cities, space is precious and, building multi-family towers is required to accommodate people who prefer to live in the city core.

You own the land and house or structure when you purchase freehold property. You decide how to maintain your home—your castle—as you please. Some people would rather own the land with freehold ownership in addition to their home; great! The age old saying goes, "we cannot make more land". There is only so much land, and some people want a small parcel to call their own. Again, there is no right or wrong answer, location and especially financial resources often influence your purchase. With a single-family home, you have no common walls with your neighbours, no elevators, and no monthly maintenance fees. All homes require maintenance so this expense is always present. Some people are adamant against paying monthly maintenance fees in a common ownership situation. I feel the pros and cons can be argued "till the cows come home." Maintenance on a single-family home can be quite high over the years. Have you priced the cost of replacing a roof recently? The cost of heating a home through North American winters can be staggering. Property taxes can make your heart skip a beat.

With freehold strata ownership, you have a set monthly maintenance fee that you are obliged to pay—no exclusions. Some people have a busy lifestyle and maintenance on a single-family home requires time that you may not have. More and more people are downsizing and younger people preferring the convenience and nightlife that a city location condominium offers.

Flipping

Do you have what it takes to be a flipper? I ask because this way of profiting from real estate requires skill and stamina. When you find an opportunity that you quickly resell, a little or a lot of updating may be required. This is commonly referred to as flipping a property. In my opinion if I purchase a property, renovate or do extensive updating and resell, this is not a flip. This of course is my own opinion. We could probably hold a town hall meeting to discuss what constitutes a flip, but that is for another time. Often picking up a property under market value does require some work to ready it for resale. You can do quite a lot to a single-family house without triggering the need for a building or alteration city permit. With strata ownership an individual owner requesting to replace original equipment is usually granted permission. If your plan is to change the flooring, replace cabinets, paint or replace some doors, replace light fixtures, these are updates that will require the blessing of the council or board when in a multi-family or strata situation. Seldom is an owner denied a reasonable request for alterations or renovations. The council and management company need to ensure renovations and alterations are being done within city and engineering guidelines for the safety of all owners and integrity of the structure. An owner may want to remove a weight bearing wall, and that is okay but support posts need to be installed to adhere to engineering specifications. This type of work requires oversight through permitting and signed off by a city inspector.

One must remember that although your intention may be to do a quick renovation and resell. Remember the building is home to dozens or maybe hundreds of owners and residents. Hours of work, cleanliness and general respect need to be kept in mind while you are there.

With a detached house, you can get going immediately on work that does not require local authority permitting. However, if you are going to alter the structure of your house by moving or eliminating a wall, any structural alterations, major plumbing, or electrical work will require a permit and inspection by your local authority. Dealing with your city permit and inspection department can take some time, but follow directions and be as accommodating as possible.

The building and development departments are typically busy places. For example, when you book an inspection at 2 p.m., it is best to be available a little before and after the time to accommodate the inspector's fluid schedule. If you miss the inspection, you will wait for the next available inspection time, and your entire project could be held up because you are required to have the *okay* to continue.

Performing work without a permit that requires a permit will come back to haunt you when you sell. If the buyer or buyer's agent approach city hall to check on any alteration work, permits are public information. If there is no permit on file for that nice new bathroom you installed in the basement, bad news, that is most likely a deal breaker. You are liable for any work performed without a permit. Your holding costs just went through the roof by having to open up newly finished walls and wait for inspection, then close up and finish. Inspectors do not rush when they know you tried to pull a fast one with no inspection.

Always expect the unexpected! You have a plan, and you are ripping apart walls when, holy crap, there are pipes in the wall that are not supposed to be there, or some crazy wiring that will now require you to have another breaker in the electrical panel to make your upgrading work safe and obtain a pass on your inspection. When you sell a property, you are responsible for its integrity, no matter what you inherited when you purchased. Renovations almost never ever go as planned, and this is just a fact of life in the renovation world. Ask any contractor or tradesperson that has worked on a renovation project. Plan for unexpected costs when preparing your budget!

On a positive note with renovating a strata title property is that there are usually not too many surprises. Typically, alterations with a condo or townhome are done within the walls of the individual suite. Strata councils and property management companies require alteration requests so that the wild west of alterations does not take place.

House owners can make alterations without the consent from anyone—a pipe gets added here, a couple extra lights get added there, or some additional venting is run above a new ceiling. The probability of running across dangerous and *not to code* alterations in a condo is not completely eliminated but substantially minimized with a strata title property.

When flipping a property, time is of the essence. You are probably paying a mortgage or interest on the line of credit you used toward the down payment and purchase your property. The return on your money is quick when flipping a house but there is the probability of more surprises. This, again, is a personal preference.

The flipper is generally a highly motivated person, often handy with tools and, or real estate savvy. The purchase price is so very important with a flip purchase. You want to be sure you have purchased below market value. You can increase the sale price only so much on upgrades alone. The pressure is on the moment the flipper takes possession. The clock is ticking to coordinate permitting, tradespeople, material ordering and dealing with the unexpected to reach the finish line. You have holding costs while doing your upgrading work so you need get in and get out in a timely fashion.

The pay-off can be rewarding in a short time with a flip project.

Secondary Suite

Obviously, you cannot have a secondary suite in a condominium. I have come across a few townhouse complexes where permission was granted for the basement to be converted to a secondary suite for rental purposes. A legal secondary suite, so far as municipal bylaws read, is required to have a private entrance. If you are comfortable sharing an entrance a relative or good friend could reside and entertain themselves in your developed basement. Kitchen and bathroom facilities could be shared on the main living level. That said, best to check your local municipal bylaws.

Secondary suites are a wonderful mortgage helper for the homeowner, and additional income for the investor. You can purchase a house where a secondary suite already exists or, typically, develop the basement area into an independent rentable space. You purchase your home, live on one level, and rent out the suite. What a great way to help with your monthly mortgage payment.

If you are an investor, you purchase a house and have two rental cheques coming to you each month—one cheque from your renter in the main living area, and one cheque from your renter in the suite portion of the house. There are many purchase opportunities where you can purchase a house with an existing suite in the basement, known as a turn-key investment opportunity. There are also situations when a previous owner installs the plumbing and doesn't go any further with developing the basement. This I call a blank canvas waiting for your renovation ideas. Find yourself a reliable contractor, a small financial investment and you have yourself a rentable suite. By owning a property like this, your renter is paying a sizable portion your mortgage. You are living in a portion of the house and your tenant is living in the suite. Or maybe all the expenses are covered by the tenants if it's a revenue property, and you put some green in your pocket at the end of the month!

Most, if not all, municipal jurisdictions now require secondary suites to be inspected and pass certain occupancy code requirements. This is for the safety of all persons living in the home. There are also some changes recently with claiming income from a secondary suite, if in your principal place of residence. Best to check with the local Municipality and an accountant so you make an informed decision.

Purchase Within Your Budget

This is worth mentioning again because, too often, I hear of people who are just scraping by each month and are not overly enthusiastic about home ownership. Do not take on more debt than is comfortable for you. Purchase in your price range that fits well within your budget to comfortably make monthly payments. Over time, you will build equity in your home; this will enable you to move up to a larger home as your family grows or the relatives move in with you.

It is the same when purchasing for investment. I continually stress cash flow or at the very least break even because if you have an unexpected situation in your suite or your building, like a fire or flood, you could be without income for a month or more. You could easily find yourself in an unfortunate situation with no rental income for some months. If your tenant is forced to temporarily move out because of flood or fire, no rental income could bring on financial hardship. The cash flow is a great way to build a cushion for the unexpected maintenance events; the hot water tank bursts, the furnace motor quits, or a sanitary service blockage are good examples of unexpected expenses that would require immediate attention.

I have known of people renting out one bedroom or more in their home for a mortgage helper, which is fine. To have tenants living in your home, is not the most desirable living situation in order to make your monthly mortgage payment. Some empty nesters or widowers need to take in some additional income in order to pay the bills that enable them to stay in their home and maintain their independents. Some young couples with small children purchase their home with the full intention to take in international language students. Homestay accommodation, as this is called is usually arranged by a homestay co-ordinator or language school where the student is attending. This enables Mom or Dad to be home for their young children while collecting an income from students to help pay the mortgage. I know of an empty nester living in a house; the kids are grown, moved away, and now raising their own families. The empty nester takes in international students, keeping her busy preparing meals, she has social time and shares

Canadian traditions and language with the young students.

Condominium or Land

"I will not own the land; my personal space is compromised; I am required to pay a monthly maintenance fee, and for what?" Everyone is entitled to their opinion, and everyone is entitled to live in whatever housing situation they choose. I say this about buyers because I have heard many reasons for and against condo ownership. At the end of the day this is a personal choice.

Owning land is fantastic. You can build what you want, within municipal guidelines of course. You can grow vegetables in the garden, install a pool, build a workshop or man cave, or have your personal equipped gym in the basement. When you own a house on a lot you decide your maintenance schedule. You are the King or Queen of your castle.

I have noticed over the past 5 years people's attitudes are softening toward condominium ownership. In larger centres, price point is such that if you want to live in the city, all you can afford is a condo in the sky or that townhouse in the suburbs. We are adaptable creatures; condominium living is something we are adapting to. Many of us grew up in a single detached home but times they are a changing. New immigrants are arriving in Canada, many from very congested and polluted cities. Many were raised and were living in a conservative sized home, often an apartment. Canada is huge; we are accustomed to wide open space and fresh air. A rite of passage, it seems almost for any young person, is to drive across Canada to experience the vast miles of forest, thousands of lakes, the mountains, and those expansive Prairie Provinces. We have been accustomed to open space, for sure. Our cities are maturing, roads are becoming congested, creating a greater need to develop transit systems, upgrade aging infrastructure, while accommodating those who want to live in the city. Building upward is the direction to go if we are to increase population in our city centres. This also increases the tax base, providing urgent needed funds for ongoing infrastructure upgrading and maintenance.

The condominium market appreciates just as detached single-family homes do. Generally, we now have a house market and a condominium market. The housing market can be rising in value while the apartment market sits stagnant. Typically, when the single detached home market reaches a price threshold, then the condominium market will become more active. So, again, when the single-family home values exceed the average buyer's budget, they adapt to purchase a townhouse or condominium unit. Home purchases then slow as condominium purchasing become more in favour. Economics 101, supply and demand dynamics then drive up condo prices. Condominium ownership is a great way for first-time buyers to enter into the market and begin building equity to eventually purchase something at a higher price point, or pay off the present mortgage and be mortgage free.

How about purchasing a condominium for your son or daughter while they attend university or college? Compare the cost of student housing in residence, or renting a suite, versus paying down a mortgage every month, and realizing property appreciation by the time they graduate. After graduation sell or gift the apartment to your newly graduated child, advertise the apartment for rent and have tenants continue paying down your mortgage. Depending on the market if you sell the unit after graduating you might profit enough that you break even with school costs. Now that is a win win! Your child receives a post-secondary education and you recoup most or all tuition costs.

A professional can guide you through the process of searching, inspecting, and purchasing a condominium. There are strata meeting minutes, AGM reports, SGM reports, Engineering reports, Building financials, and a home inspection report to review when looking to purchase a condominium.

The reality is that condominium ownership is affordable for many people. In larger cities owning a single-family home is beyond reach for the average young couple. If lifestyle is your driving force and you enjoy the action of the city centre then freehold strata ownership is for you. Young families will buy in outlying areas where home ownership is attainable. Owning in a more affordable area could mean a longer commute, but if you want to raise your family in a single detached home this could be your reality. Some young couples will start with the purchase of a condo, build up some equity and by the time they are starting a family they have some equity from selling the condo to put toward the purchase of a house. The biggest idea I am stressing is get into the market! Over time real estate has been the best investment so buy something and get yourself into the market! Do not be a nay-sayer waiting for real estate to crash and property values decrease by 50%, it's not going to happen. Wow, this is getting better! You are tired of this old house—renovate or sell? I have great stuff to tell you, so keep reading.

Notes

Notes

Sell or Renovate

Why Do You Want to Sell?

So, the old place has lost its charm. The days of feeling excited when you pull up in the driveway have withered. Perhaps the kids have grown and moved out, the cabinets and flooring are outdated, and the peach coloured tub and toilet just are not doing it for you anymore.

You are thinking of a change. You are obviously familiar with the neighbourhood, you are friendly with the neighbours, and you have memories in the old place. Maybe you are thinking it is time to downsize to a new home that is more manageable to maintain. Maybe you want to diversify your investing portfolio, or you want your money to work a little harder for you. I will get into that in the next section.

Living in a new area with new surroundings, in a newer home, has its appeal. Maybe you would like to live closer to work and amenities, so that you can leave your car at home more often.

Another option is to renovate your present home to give it a fresh new contemporary look and feel. New cabinets and lighting in the kitchen, new tiles, new vanity and lighting in the bathroom, maybe change out the closet bi-fold doors for mirror sliders can brighten and transform the space to contemporary decorating scheme—for the kitchen, new appliances, updated cabinets with some nice hardware, counter tops finished in granite or a manufactured quartz stone with backspace tiling. Perhaps some nice engineered hardwood, laminate flooring in the living area, and fresh ceramic tile in the kitchen, finished with a 4 to 6 inch-high profile baseboard throughout the house, gives a nice updated look. Those interesting light fixtures you have seen could be installed, and maybe the chandelier you have always loved could make its new home in your dining area. How about the outside landscaping? Would you like to have a landscaping company create that raised garden bed, and plant that blossoming cherry tree you have always wanted? Oh, and some new sod, and maybe resurface the driveway. The costs associated with selling, re-buying, and some minor alterations in your new home, could be put into updating your existing home to give it a fresh and updated look. Most worthy of mention is that painting your home is the cheapest and most effective way to change the look and feel of your home. There are many studies you can find online with the results of the effect that colour has on our mood. A fresh coat of paint throughout your home gives it a fresh new look.

Getting into large scale renovations of your home is not to be entered into without some planning and a budget. Some items that can be replaced without a large scale renovation are: counter tops, cabinets, flooring, painting, lighting, mouldings, electrical receptacles and switches, and tiling. Go ahead, investigate and maybe invest in the services of a decorator for half a day and see what ideas and rough pricing they can come up with.

Home Equity-Leveraging Investing Options

With real estate, leverage is our friend. You put down 20% of the cost of a home and you gain the appreciation on 100% of the value! This is the same when purchasing investment property. You invest 20% as a down payment and you collect rental income on 100% of the value! This is so important for you to understand. Find material online you can read so that you can gain a deeper understanding and appreciation of leveraging. (www.you2canownrealestate.com)

You have options before you: remortgage your existing home, taking out some equity for a down payment on your next principal residence. Rent out your existing home and move into your new home. Ideally the rent income is more than enough to continue paying the mortgage and all monthly expenses with a surplus, known as your cash flow. The cash flow from your, now rental property, can go toward a maintenance fund, or put down additional cash on the mortgage of your new personal residence to pay it down quicker. This is how equity and leveraging is our friend when investing. Now, all expenses are paid on the rental property, you have a cash surplus each month, and the property value will be going up, on average, 3% a year. Do the math on this, and you will see an amazing return on your money every year. It does not matter if the market is fluctuating because all your rental property expenses are covered, glorious!

You always have options with real estate. Sometimes you need to seek advice outside your sphere of influence. The average person deals with a couple of real estate transactions in a lifetime. It is okay to ask for advice from a qualified person. Every one of us cannot possibly know all there is to know about everything. Pain and discomfort are good motivators but making a bad investment choice can hurt your financial situation for years. Real estate is a great investment but the market turns slowly and changing investing directions cannot be done instantly as compared to a stock investment. Do not be a lone wolf and do not be too proud to ask for the opinion of someone with experience.

So, another option can be for you to sell the old place. With the funds from the sale you then purchase a couple condo properties—one to live in and one to rent. This option is good if you are downsizing and looking for hands-off management of your rental property and a maintenance free personal residence—taking care of lawns, weeding gardens, cleaning gutters, shoveling snow, exterior window cleaning and general upkeep. Townhouse or condo living can be relaxing, being that you are not always doing some kind of maintenance to the property. The monthly fee generally pays for the daily upkeep and maintenance of the complex.

Investing your equity into condo ownership for rental purposes can be done with minimal hands on maintenance required. As mentioned previously, all maintenance to common property is managed by the property management company, using the funds contributed, known as the strata fees, from all owners in the complex. You are responsible for maintenance within the walls of your unit.

Another option could be for you to stay in your home. Renovate it for a fresh, updated look. You can install a secondary suite in the basement to receive rental income.

You take out some equity from your home, to purchase another house or a condo as an investment property. So you continue living in your home, using leverage to purchase a rental property and now the tenants rent covers the new mortgage payments.

Now, the renter in the basement suite is essentially paying the equity back to the bank that you took out to purchase your investment property. The investment property should be cash flowing (money left over at the end of the month after all expenses are paid). Remember, revenue property expenses are the mortgage, property tax, utilities, insurance, and property management fees. Add all the annual costs together, then divide by 12 (months) to arrive at your monthly cost. So, now your investment property is financially supporting itself. You could hire a property management company that will find a tenant, collect rent and generally look after your rental property, dealing with the tenant and any other issues. You are consulted when extraordinary events arise. You arrange with the management company when you are to be notified of any events occurring at your property. Some owners will give permission to the management company to take care of any repairs under a pre-determined amount, let's say $300, without needing your pre-authorization.

I have explained only a few of the many ways and many options how you can structure your investing dollars into real estate. Anything new can seem confusing but go over your options a couple times with perhaps a mortgage broker that deals with investors. A realtor you trust. A co-worker or family member that owns investment property. Ask them how they leverage their money to purchase. Ask them how they came to arrive at their present investing situation. Ask them about any mistakes they made along the way. Ask them if they knew then what they know now, what would they have done different. My purpose with this book is to create the interest to own and invest in real estate. You need continue to ask questions and gather information.

Costs Related to Selling vs. Renovating

You might be looking at a permanent work transfer to another city or you are downsizing, perhaps retired, then selling may be your best option. There can come a time when it is time to sell. I am only providing options for building your investment portfolio. If and when you downsize, it is prudent to still invest your money wisely. You worked hard for what you have and you also want your money to work for you. When it is time to sell this old house you will be rewarded by a substantially larger selling price compared to when you purchased. Property appreciation has probably been kind to you.

If you decide to sell, you are going to invest time and money to ready your property for sale— perhaps paint high-traffic areas, hallways, kitchen, and do some minor outside sprucing up. You want to ensure your property has curb appeal. "Curb appeal?" you might ask. When a prospective buyer drives up for the first time in front of your home, the appearance of your property is important for the prospect buyer when they drive up for the first time and have that first impression. First impressions are important and, if a prospect buyer likes what they see walking up, then you are well on your way to a sale. Purchasing a home is an emotional experience; having a good feeling when they initially roll up to your home will help to influence their buying decision. Remember that pride of home ownership you had when you first purchased this old place? The new owner will desire this same feeling. They need to see themselves living in your home. Spending some money getting the gardens looking neat, lawns trimmed, and some paint splashed on the house exterior will go a long way toward first impressions. What is commonly referred to as *lipstick,* or cosmetic updates, will attract more people to view your home and, in turn, a quicker sale. The average person today can research on their own; part of that is looking at photos on the MLS system. A fresh and bright look from new paint and a tidy property attracts buyers.

From the proceeds of the sale the Realtor is paid. Check with the real estate board in your area for commission rates. Your new home may require some upgrades—flooring, paint, plumbing, or lighting fixtures. Then, when you purchase another home you will pay property transfer tax to the government, when buying—1% on first $200,000; 2% on amount $200,000 – $2,000,000; 3% on amount greater than $2,000,000. On an $800,000 purchase you would pay $14,000 for property purchase tax, $2,000 on the first 200K and $12,000 on the remaining 600K. So safe to say you spend $50-60K by the time you settle into your new home. If you are purchasing a revenue property, those costs are an expense that go against your income for the year. Speak with an accountant for up to date and relevant information on revenue property.

The option here is to renovate your existing home using the 50–60K toward the cost of updating. Renovating would give your home a fresh new look with the finishing touches of your choice. When you buy a property new, you get what the builder installed. Do you like the large format tile around the shower and bath tub installed in show homes and display centres? The cabinets that you have always loved? That dark mahogany flooring that would look sleek in your workspace or office? The open kitchen concept you could achieve by removing a wall? With renovating, you can make all the changes you want—within local building codes, of course. You want to open up the layout and remove that wall between the dining room and the kitchen? Now is the time you can make those changes, giving your home, and maybe yourself as well, a fresh start, a new perspective on things! Having the skilled people to manage your renovations is strongly recommended. Depending on the extent and depth of your upgrades, you may want to move to one level of your home while the work is in progress.

When taking on a large scale renovation the need for thorough planning and then more planning cannot be stressed enough. Your home is pretty much upside down, a construction zone for the duration of the work. Maybe this is a good time to reconnect with a relative, or move back in with Mom and Dad for a while. The satisfaction of a newly renovated home is so gratifying. Firstly you will be relieved because the work is finally complete, and secondly experience new found pleasure with the transformation of your home. An overwhelming feeling of pride of ownership will once again be yours when you arrive home, sit in your big armchair, and survey your beautiful new home!

Mortgage Helper

I touched on secondary suites earlier but I feel this is worthy of another mention. You love your home, your neighbours are fantastic, and you want to stay right where you are—good! Your kids, who once ran around the house, have since purchased property of their own and raising families of their own. You've been thinking about all the space you have in the house now. You'd like some space for when the grandchildren come to visit. How about creating a rental suite in the basement? "Oh, but," you say, "I do not want tenants walking through my living space." There may already be a private entrance for the tenant or you can create one. If your laundry room is in the basement, you can make the laundry room common space for you and your tenant, or purchase a nice compact stacking washer/dryer for either yourself or your tenant; that way, you both have private laundry.

The income received from a 2-bedroom suite will change your lifestyle or cover the expenses of traveling that you have always wanted to do. By having a tenant living in a lower suite, someone is around the property when you are away. If you are a snowbird, or are often away, there is always activity around your property. (www.you2canownrealestate.com)

Your basement may already have a washroom, bedroom, and activity room, which, with some additional work, could be converted to a self-contained secondary suite. Having the income from a secondary suite can enable you to stay in your home if you have a limited income. Rental income assists homeowners with the paying of mortgage, property taxes and other expenses. Creating a secondary suite is a viable way to stay in your home while receiving monthly income from your tenant.

If you could realize an additional $500–$1,500 or more a month, that is $6,000–$18,000 per year; would it be worth your time to investigate creating a suite? Depending on the city and neighbourhood you live in, or the size of suite, you could be earning much more than what I have quoted per month.

Certainly, in my mind, it is worth investigating if you are looking for an additional stream of income or wanting to pay down your mortgage, or to purchase more property. Money is not everything, although it can make life more comfortable. My hope is to provide some alternatives for easing your financial obligation to the bank each month, or if you owe little or no mortgage, a secondary suite could generate a nice income stream.

Some new tax regulations are being developed around earning income from a secondary suite. It is best to check with your accountant and federal tax authority.

Are you having difficulty sitting still? We have just compared some pros and cons of selling versus renovating. Let's still look a little deeper into renovations. Does the thought of turning your home upside down excite you? Terrify you? The next section will prepare you to be the renovator you have always wanted to be, or not!

Notes

Notes

Notes

Dealing with Contractors, Tradespeople and Liabilities

Are You Qualified to Operate Power Tools?

Get ready for the ride! So, you have decided to renovate your personal residence, construct a secondary suite, do some updates in your rental property, or maybe you have found a great *fix and flip* opportunity. Strap on your seatbelt and get ready for the ride. Whatever the work ahead of you, be open to change; expect surprises and know that every day of construction gets you closer to completion.

You plan to do the work yourself, or with a friend or family member. Alternatively, you may have absolutely no desire to operate power tools or roll paint onto the wall. We are all good at something, but doing renovation work just may not be your area of expertise. If you are planning more extensive renovations, for example removing a wall or replacing bathtub or shower where multiple trades are required, you will want to consider hiring a contractor or tradespersons.

I remember viewing a house in mild shock some years ago that was listed for sale. In the listing description, it read, "Recently renovated throughout." The owner had done all the work himself. Unfortunately, the owner was unable to see that all the work he did was unfinished, and the workmanship was less than would be expected for the advertised renovated home listing. No exaggeration—most of the work would need to be ripped out and redone. Some of the updates could be repaired or salvaged to be acceptable. Any possible buyer who viewed the home would immediately notice the poor finishing, and would be thinking of the time and money they would need to spend to get the house up to "just renovated" condition. In regard to selling, the owner would have been better to have left the home in its original condition versus such poor workmanship. The owner did his best, but doing renovation work is not for novices if you want to sell the property. A house is a man's castle and he will do as he pleases. When selling, you need to think as a buyer and what they would think if they were walking through this home for the first time. His money would have been better spent nicely updating the bathroom or kitchen where he would realize a return on his money. The take away here is to be realistic about your renovating skills and abilities.

If you are not in a rush to complete the work, and your life is not disrupted with the job unfinished, you can often get a better price for services rendered by a contractor or tradesperson. They will work on your home between other larger projects as sort of a filler during slow times, for them.

A lower overall cost for renovations are realized when you update multiple rooms versus updating one room now and one room next year. We all have some financial constraints but, if your budget allows only updating part of your house now and the remainder later, then that is okay.

There are thousands of instructional videos on YouTube for any and every type of renovation work. If you are a handy person and you want to do your own renovations just take your time, watch how the professionals do it and replicate the process. Accept that you will make mistakes, and expect the unexpected.

Considerations – Freehold vs. Condominium

Freehold and condominium (freehold strata) ownership are two completely different animals. In your single detached home, go ahead and change whatever you like—rip out walls, change plumbing, install electrical receptacles, change flooring, and work early in the morning or late into the night without interruption. You can hire whomever you want to do the work for you, no problem. You just go to your local city hall, apply for a building or alteration permit if required, do the work, have it inspected, and enjoy your beautifully updated home.

Okay, so now you want to do some updates to your strata unit. You are required to submit in writting to the council and property management company a list of alterations you plan on doing. Structural considerations and limitations of alterations are enforced in a condominium building. The integrity of the building needs to be maintained for the health and safety of all owners. The council works on behalf of all the owners and gives the final aye or nay to the alteration requests. If a wall is to be removed or altered, you must first check if it is a load bearing wall. Some buildings only allow a selected plumbing companies to do any plumbing work in the building. Some buildings only allow one company to work within the building because they are intimately familiar with the building. The idea is that having one company doing any plumbing work minimizes the possibility of poor work- manship and, if anything goes sideways, the company will know exactly what has been done in the building. Strata complexes make rules like this because of previous poor workmanship.

Strata or property management councils seldom refuse reasonable renovation requests. Correspondence may go back and forth a few times with additional questions being asked or some items being in need of clarification. As the owner of a strata unit, you own and are responsible for everything within the walls of your unit. Altering anything in the walls, be it plumbing or electrical, requires the consent of the council. Updates performed within your unit, and found to be dangerous, not to building code, or unauthorized in any way will likely be in contravention to the bylaws. You may be asked to remove, change back to the original condition or, worse, be on the hook for damages and repairs for a flood or fire caused by your poor workmanship. An owner is liable for any updating work within a suite.

When you have received the blessing of the council, you can move full speed ahead with your renovations. Loud noise related to renovation work can usually be made between the hours clearly written in the buildings bylaws. Cleaning of debris and moving material in and out of the building should be reviewed at the start of your work. You have neighbours that appreciate quiet when they are at home after a day of work. I know from experience that it is easy to continue working into the evening hours; you want to finish a project versus leaving a small amount for the morning. Like I say, unforeseen things can happen: start time of the tiling project was late;

the cement is on the floor and the work must continue. I just bring this to your attention, but you will make the call when you find yourself in such a situation, because you will be presented with unforeseen delays and surprises.

You want the building onsite maintenance person to be your friend. On one occasion I was beginning a renovation in a concrete high-rise. Initially the onsite maintenance person was grumpy and probably viewed me as another guy coming in to make a mess and generally needed to be watched. I was replacing the white appliances with stainless steel, and asked him if he knew anyone needing a working fridge or stove. His daughter just happened to be in need of a newer fridge. He was my best friend for the duration of the project. During another project, I took the time to chat with and get to know the onsite person. Again I offered the appliances. They did not know anyone but the consideration went a long way.

Be respectful of others living in the building, it's their home. It is easy to get wrapped up in the busyness of a renovation and only want to cross the finish line. Working late into the evening, leaving the hallways dirty and littered with debris, transporting demolition debris in the elevator without protection on the walls. Put yourself in the position of an owner in the building and what would be acceptable to you?

My intention is not to instill fear into you when working in a strata or condominium complex. Renovations are being done in condominiums every day. These buildings create bylaws for the protection and safety of all owners. Read and be familiar with the bylaws before you begin your project. There are more hoops to jump through when dealing with strata property but this is just how it is.

Hiring a Contractor and Trades People

So, you have chosen to move ahead with your renovation project. The scope of work is quite large, or you may not have the time to set aside from your regular life to take it on yourself. A contractor will get the work completed quicker compared to you doing the work on weekends and evenings.

If you have a limited funds to work with, do some investigation and research what type of finishings you like and work it into your overall budget. For example, the type of flooring, cabinets, counter top, sinks, faucets, lights, doors, and paint. If your budget allows, hire a designer to guide you through this process. You will appreciate the finished product and avoid work stoppages while you decide what product or material to move ahead with. I have hired a designer to come in for a one-time consultation and leave me with a variety of colours and materials to choose from going forward. This is inexpensive but requires a comfort level to choose material and match colours in materials to achieve flow in the finish product.

Interview a couple or more contractors. Walk through your home with them, describing what you want to do. Ask for a written cost estimate for work to be done, usually honored for 60 or 90 days. The cost of materials and labour can fluctuate, so estimates do change. How busy a contractor is can also influence the cost of work. If a contractor is not busy, and needs to keep his guys working, you will generally receive a cheaper price compared to the busy season when there is more work around than he or she can do.

Ask the contractor for photos of his previous jobs completed and any letters of recommendation from past customers. A contractor that takes the time to document his or her work, has pride in their work and is proud to show the world. Do not fear asking for a copy of liability insurance, WCB, and a business licence that enables them to work in your city. Accidents do happen and, if you have a contractor and his crew working in your home, you want all documentation in place.

When working on a condominium, hiring contractors with insurance is imperative. I have seen more than once the puncture of a waterline by mistake. Once, the carpet layer was hammering his smooth edge down around the perimeter of the room. The hot water heating line was tucked in the corner where the floor met the wall. When he hammered the nail into the floor to fasten the smooth edge, he drove the nail into the water line, under pressure, shooting hot water across the room! The building manager just happened to be in another area of the building doing an inspection; he was able to turn off the water to the suite within 10–15 minutes. In a different situation I watched as my hired plumber used his torch to solder a copper pipe in my wall—the old, dry wood stud caught on fire! The water is turned off because we have the plumbing system opened up and I have the beginning of a fire in my wall, yikes! Fortunately we had some drinking water bottles on hand and quickly put the fire out. These are just a couple of examples of things that happen during the course of a renovation project. Water and fire are essential for our survival but very destructive when out of control in our living environment. A large condominium building can have multiple suites damaged when a water leak is undetected or cannot be shut down immediately.

If you are taking a more hands-on approach and hiring tradespeople directly, then it is best that you check with your insurance agent for the best way to protect yourself against any liability.

Managing Your Renovation Project

The first few renovation projects I took on were a huge learning curve. When the place was gutted, I clearly remember an unsettled feeling in the pit of my stomach and thinking "What have I done?" Do not fear the renovation; one way or another, you will get the job done.

If you are taking on the work yourself, just be clear with yourself your abilities and limitations. We all enjoy to save a dollar but, at the end of the day, you are forever legally liable for the work you do—yes, forever, or you die, whichever comes first.

You want to keep open a good line of communication with your contractor and tradespeople. There is a fine line between keeping the contractor informed and telling him how to do his job. At the end of the day, of course, you are the boss, and you want the tradesperson on your side. There are many moving parts to your renovation project, so you want to check in with your contractor daily. There are many small changes and decisions that need to be made as the project progresses, and you want to be part of the decision making process. I experienced the tradesperson make decisions for me while I was out of country on vacation. His intention was honorable thinking he was saving time and keeping the project moving. The change from the original plan was not what I would have chosen; I then had to alter future finishing and design because the overall plan had changed. Your contractor and tradespersons do not think like you; he or she does not have your tastes or the overall vision for the finished product. Sometimes a compromise is required between what you want and what can be done.

There will be changes to the original plan, so do not be surprised. For example, wires are in the wall that were not on any plan, or plumbing in walls is not up to code. Houses have more surprises compared to a condominium. You may have delays because one of the trades cannot continue his work until the trade before him finishes their work. For example the tiler cannot do his work until the plumber installs the shower. The painter cannot paint until the drywaller has completed installing, mudding and sanding the wall. Larger contractors have multiple job sites that fluctuate needs for labour and type of trades required on different sites each day. A contractor may prioritize work on another larger site for a day or so before returning to your project.

Whatever amount you budget for your renovation, a 10% reserve fund is general rule of thumb when budgeting a project. There will be unexpected work required that the contractor could not have known about until tearing apart a wall or ripping up a floor. Extra and additional time by the contractor will be extra cost to you. One common extra is leveling a floor before installing laminate or hardwood flooring.

Be fair to your tradespeople, but do not be taken advantage of. Like any profession, some people promise the world but fall short in their delivery. There are enough horror stories out there of people unsatisfied with the work they received. Minimize the chance of you having a horror story to tell co-worker and relatives for years by checking out a contractor the best you can before hiring him or her for a large project.

You are now more familiar with renovating and dealing with contractors—not a walk in the park but not rocket science either. You can do it! Hold on; there is more coming in this next chapter for you to act on: what type of investor are you, or want to be. This is very important when making your buying decisions!

Notes

Notes

Notes

What Type of Investor Are You?

Your Risk Tolerance

There is no right or wrong with your level of risk tolerance. There are some definite do's and don'ts when investing but, as far as your level of risk, you need to decide, and you will have determined this through past experience or future ventures.

For example, a revenue property, occupied by respectful and financially secure tenants, is a safe and steady *as you go* investment. Your mortgage is being paid down every month, and your property value is appreciating over time—a fantastic low risk investment. Families have accumulated great wealth over time by applying this very formula. Patience and time works for you. You eventually will have debt-free property to pass down to your children. As long as you teach them investing principles, they will continue building wealth with these investments. Money invested into a secondary suite in your home is extremely low risk and a superb mortgage helper. If you are more of a risk-taker and are looking for a quicker return on your money, you may want to purchase a pre-sale property. Typically, condominiums are sold before the ground is broken to erect the tower. You can purchase any number of units with the anticipation the market will continue to rise. In a rising market you can sell the contract to another buyer for more than you paid. This works best when there is more demand than product, creating a rise in market value. If the market turns downward while you own this property, you need to be prepared to secure a mortgage or sell at a loss. If you plan to rent out your pre-sale unit, then the following applies: the developer has your deposit, usually 10–25% of the total purchase price, for approximately 3 years until the project is complete. When your suite is ready to occupy, you advertise for a renter. If the market has continued to rise since you signed the contract, the value of your condominium will be higher and you have increased your net worth. If the market slides down from the time you signed the contract to purchase and completion date then follow the same steps to find a tenant, rent out the suite and eventually values will rise again. Remember your mortgage is always being paid down every month. Another slightly risky way of investing is building a spec house. This is purchasing a house or empty lot, tearing it down, and rebuilding a new house to sell at a profit. Again, as long as market conditions stay the same, or is increasing, this works well. If the market experiences a correction and values drop while you are building, you need to be prepared to rent the house to pay the mortgage, or sell at a loss. Depending on the region you live, the rent for a new home may or may not cover all your monthly expenses.

There are so many more ways to invest in real estate, but I have only highlight a few for you here. (www.you2canownrealestate.com)

Shark, Fix and Flip, Buy and Hold

Are you a *shark* investor? Would you like to find your deals from hard luck situations? For example, a marriage breakup or separation where the couple needs to liquidate quickly, selling below market value; a family did not recover from being unemployed for a time and need to sell quickly to avoid defaulting on their mortgage; a struggling business owner requires capital and is selling his or her home to inject cash into their business. There are estate sales, bankruptcies, job transfer, mental illness, FSBO selling below market value. These are but a few examples of situations in where investors can minimize the seller's loss and, or just find a good deal. There are ways the advanced investor can become a joint venture partner and become part owner of a property when the owner is struggling. The investor can inject cash or take over mortgage payments; in return, the struggling individual pays the investor rent and, after an agreed upon length of time, the investor is then paid a fee for bailing out the home owner, or the property is sold, and the investor is entitled to a portion of the funds from the sale. Each of this type of investor opportunity needs to be assessed carefully because each individual opportunity will be unique and will require a creative structure and an eventual exit.

Are you a *fix and flipper?* Do you enjoy renovating?

Do you have a crew to do property updates? Can you mobilize and be very busy for a short time? If yes, then maybe you want to buy an original condition house or condo, do a quick renovation, and sell it. Time is of the essence when doing fix and flips. How much is the money costing you that you used for down payment? If you used your line of credit, you might be paying prime, plus half a percent on the borrowed funds, in addition to a monthly mortgage payment. You will have your closing costs when you take possession, renovation costs, mortgage payments for as long as you hold the property, and real estate commission fees when you sell. Generally, you need to be quick with these types of projects. You do not have the luxury to only work on weekends with a project like this. You need to pass the start gate running as soon as you take possession and have the keys. Some pre-planning will save much time once renovations have begun. Remember, you make your money the day you purchase. The market sets the selling price of property. The only thing you can control is how much you pay for a property. So, when you purchase a property for 10% below market value, you just made your money the day you bought. You cannot purchase a property at market value, spend $50,000 on renovations, and expect to make money. Add up your closing costs, renovation costs, and commission fees—you just donated money to keeping the economy stimulated. Properties come available frequently that can be fixed and flipped for profit. You need to be patient, and always looking. Tell everyone what you are looking for; have a real estate agent working for you who understands and appreciates investors.

Are you a *buy and hold* investor? You have an investment property, and maybe several properties rented to quality tenants. You make repairs when needed to keep your quality tenants happy. You receive steady rental income that is paying all your expenses, paying down your mortgage, and putting some change in your pocket every month. Over time, your property increases in value and, eventually, you have a mortgage free property. When mortgage free, you have the equivalent to a money tree. Use the cash flow to invest in more property, take a family vacation, do whatever you like with this additional income stream. Maybe you purchase a unit for your son or daughter to live in while they study at a post-secondary institution. The mortgage gets paid down versus you paying dormatory fees. When their post-secondary studies are completed, you may want to gift the unit to them, advertise it for rent, or sell.

REITs, Limited Partnership, Ownership Within Rental Pool

So, you believe in the growth potential of real estate over time; you want to invest in real estate and are looking for investing options. You may be looking for a more hands-off investing approach, one being REITs. This is short for Real Estate Investment Trust. You invest into a commercial real estate REIT, residential REIT, retail REIT, or mortgage REIT. This investing product is often RRSP, RESP, and TFSA friendly. You want to perform your due diligence to investigate historical returns, past performance of the fund, the strength and history of the management. Returns are not guaranteed so it's best to contact a financial advisor for more detailed information and direction with this type of investing.

Limited partnership is another investing vehicle where, again, you invest with a developer in a project; there is a start and end date often the length of time required to get permitting in place, construct the building and sell the units. Have your lawyer or financial advisor investigate the company history and the type of product being invested in; for example, construction of a condominium complex or the purchase of one or a number of multi-family rental buildings. There are companies that invest strictly in Canada or strictly in the US or invest in both countries. Some investment funds are shares in the entire company portfolio, some investment opportunity is for a specific building and for a specific amount of time. An example would be interest payments paid to you annually with your entire investment returned at the end of five years. There are a variety of interest payment and equity repayment schedules unique to each individual investment. Again, have your accountant or lawyer review any investment so you go in with your eyes wide open. A second opinion is priceless when investing your hard earned money!

Multi-Family Buildings

You have been investing for a while, you have the knowledge and drive to step up your investing and you want to purchase a multi-family rental building. This is an entirely different scale of investing, which is very rewarding. For you more novice investors, financing criteria and qualifications for a mortgage for this type of product are different compared to buying a house, duplex, or condominium unit. The bank or lender analyses the building financials, physical condition and compares the purchase price to the assessed value. The ability for the building income to cover all expenses is also important. You will often hear people speak of the capitalization rate or "cap rate" when referring to the value of a multi-family building. The most basic way to describe cap rate is the net operating income (gross income – operating costs = net income) divided by the purchase price to arrive at a percentage value is the cap rate. The individual(s) financial fitness purchasing the multi-family building will be taken into consideration but a building financials and assessment value are a major factor when financing. In comparison, when purchasing a house or condominium unit, the lender mostly takes into consideration your personal ability to service the debt although assessed value is always a factor. Your personal home does not generate income so this is generally why your financial health and income plays an important role with getting qualified for your mortgage.

There is so much more involved with purchasing multi-family buildings that I will not go into here. Many experienced commercial realtors, seasoned investors and the good old internet are a great source for you to collect more information.

New Home Builder

You have always loved the smell of lumber, maybe you enjoy building things and want to build a house—another fantastic way to earn income through real estate!

You will need to purchase a lot to build on, or maybe you want to stay in the neighbourhood and rebuild on your existing lot. If you are purchasing a vacant lot, you will be required to qualify under the residential mortgage rules using the debt servicing method. You can also find some lenders who will lend against the property value, as a commercial loan with fees attached. So, now you have secured your building lot; you have house plans designed to your specific needs and a budget worked out. Typically, you will hire a builder and he will manage all the sub-trades and building details. The bank or lender will advance you a cash draw at specific stages of completion. This money enables you to pay your builder and continue with your project. The joy of this is that you do not require all cash up front for the building costs. You want to have some sort of contingency fund to draw on for items not covered by the banks cash advances. Remember that 10% contingency, or the "I was not expecting that" fund I mentioned earlier? You want to have some cash to draw from to pay for the unexpected when building.

When your building is completed, you should now have a house valued for more than your costs of purchasing the lot and building the house. You could have built a secondary suite that becomes your mortgage helper. A new secondary suite commands top dollar in your area. You can live on the upper floors, rent out the lower portion, or sell the entire house for a profit. If you build with the purpose to sell and the real estate market experiences a correction while you are building, then be prepared to put renters in the house to cover costs until the market rebounds. You could also move into the house yourself, or sell to break even or maybe at a small loss. It would be a shame to invest time and finances then sell at a loss. Always have a plan B!

Notes

Notes

Investors Stay Focused

Birds of a Feather Flock Together

Seasoned investors hang around and meet with other investors who are taking action and making deals happen. You are probably somewhere between looking to purchase your first piece of real estate and being a well-heeled investor. The way to learn about investing techniques is to be around other experienced investors who are making deals happen. Search for public investing groups in your area that may meet up on a regular schedule and offer education and support for the budding investor. There may be a monthly fee to become a member, but it is well worth the knowledge and possible earning potential. Beware of the traveling real estate show that is coming to your town. Often they sell you an unrealistic formula to become wealthy with real estate. Always remember the fundamentals. Real estate goes up over time. Don't look for a get rich quick scheme by leveraging your credit cards with thousands of dollars. The Joe Shmoe that is going to teach you his investing secrets in one weekend is a shmuck and will only influence you to spend money on his system. This is not investing, not even careless investing but rather donating your money to a traveling road show. Often these guys are selling a dream with no substance. Please do not be fooled by the promise of making thousands in the next month. I personally know successful investors that started out spending tens of thousands of dollars on expensive programs to earn money from real estate. After failing with the high paid system they learned that following the time tested methods of investing cost only their time to learn how other investors became successful. Whenever have you heard of anyone, with anything be successful by purchasing a get rich quick secret formula.

I have some dear friends who own their home but, when I am talking in detail about real estate investing, a blank look comes across their face. They are kind to listen to my story or adventure but are not really interested to discuss the intimacies of real estate investing. Many friends and family enjoy listening to my adventures and some do not share my passion for real estate. They are very interesting people, raising their families, contributing to their community, and generally living a full life. They would much rather talk about their child's soccer accomplishment or an escape to a tropical location or how our local sports teams are doing. That is all good; these people enrich my life as I do theirs.

You want to be discussing real estate investing with investor friends and other professionals in the business. These people will widen your knowledge about how to structure deals, where to find deals, what has worked well for them, and some pitfalls to avoid. Learning from others mistakes is priceless. Ask questions—lots of questions—and after you ask a question, shut up and listen. I know from experience, enthusiasm for investing and wanting to share my opinion can impede my ability to hear. Active investors do not listen to the media hype and do not dwell on it by discussing and obsessing over it. Like exercising in the gym, you will develop investor muscles. You will learn to identify opportunity and what to do when you see it.

An investor's motivation and drive is difficult to maintain when you're out there alone trying to figure everything out by yourself. Believe me you need to be plugged in and on your game so you are prepared to take action when a deal comes along. To scan the MLS listings, and go out on a rainy night to look at property, can seem pretty drab if you do not have the anticipation that your next deal could be the next property you view. Finding the deal is often about timing; so, when you hear of a possible deal, you need to spring to action, immediately! Having the attitude that you are tired and you will give them a call on the weekend or next week produces nothing. You will come across a property or deal that seems good, but you are not entirely sure and need a professional opinion. This is where having a network of investors and experienced real estate professionals can help you. You come across a great deal and are thinking to purchase to fix and flip, but you need to act quickly to secure the property at such a low price. What do you do? Well, first call your preferred real estate agent for a professional opinion and write an offer to secure the property. You will have a week to do your due diligence on the property, work out your costs, establish the selling price and you will know if there is profit in the deal or not. There are so many scenarios of how to obtain a real estate opportunity. You must know the product you are searching for so you can quickly spot opportunity! The knowledge of investing goes deep. The more you learn and hang around other real estate enthusiasts, the better investor you become. We may be living in the best time in history for the average person to accumulate wealth through real estate. Investing knowledge is priceless and this knowledge will enable you to build your real estate portfolio and eventually increase your personal net worth beyond your wildest dreams!

Media Hype

As a real estate investor, you need to sift through media reports to separate fact from fiction. The media is necessary and plays an important role to investigate and report news. Unfortunately, real estate articles gets recycled, an opinion piece, and is often yesterday's news. Real estate markets are in a constant state of flux, and the media hype has a heyday with the headlines. Your head will be spinning and confusion will ensue: reading about an opinion piece predicting the bubble is going to burst; sales are 10% less this month compared to same month last year; market is short on inventory; sale price up from last month but lower from same month last year; prices are above the ten year average; prices are below the ten year average. Statistics are important and necessary to identify trends and the health of the markets. There are many different stats reported and you need to listen clearly what is being said and obtain all the information before going into panic mode or thinking you have missed the boat. The media just has too much influence playing on people's emotions with the big splashy headlines. Often, the headlines seem to read that the boat has left the dock and you missed it, or you made it on the boat and are out in open water, but the boat has developed a leak and is sinking—yikes. Read between the lines, my investing friends; become truly informed so you can identify fact from fiction! Staying close to other investors is key for you to be disciplined and stick to the basics. Your increased investor knowledge will enable you to identify articles as entertainment because you will know what is really happening out there. For investment property, stick to the basics, you can buy property in any market and have the tenant's rent cover all the expenses. Your local real estate board publishes monthly statistics on number of listings, number of sales, average pricing, and pricing compared to previous months. Be open to learn new investing strategies from those who have gone before you. Patience, determination and confidence are required to be a successful investor. Successful investors are the minority and investors do not get caught up in the negative conversation that real estate is crazy, so expensive, becoming unaffordable. These attitudes may reflect some true but stick to the basics and there is always opportunity. The rewards are well worth your time. It is a steep learning curve and as you learn about investing in real estate you will know if you want to continue learning more to become a more experienced investor. You need to seek out real estate investing groups, professionals, and other investors to discuss and learn more about investing. There are many good books, including this one, which will help propel you to the next level of real estate investing.

Again, the media reports the news, and they need to sell papers and subscriptions; sensational real estate headlines are what sells. Hyped-up news articles play on people's emotions, and that equals sales and the survival of news outlets. Choose your news source carefully. There is available quality and up to date reporting about real estate, and current local and world events that affect pricing and market stability. You can always find real estate deals, no matter what market and no matter what area. Do not be guided by the hype!

The best opportunity is to buy before a market goes up. I have not yet found a crystal ball to predict every market before it rises. There are certain determinants that are necessary for an area to be up and coming. Be informed and you will know how to identify undervalued real estate. When a market has been rising for a while and everyone, including Aunt Bessy, is buying real estate for investment, this is a dangerous time to buy - when you are feeling you need to get into the market before you get left behind. The market has probably reached its peak by this time. One of my real estate mentors always says the markets become what people are talking about. Buyer's confidence or lack of confidence will turn a market.

Desires, Dreams, Goals

Okay, so you might be saying, "Here we go with goal setting; reading them before I go to bed, and again upon awakening, motivational phrases on my fridge, on the bathroom mirror." If you are that motivated, you go, champ; you will develop a lifestyle beyond belief. For most of us *on again, off again* goal setters, I want to quickly bring to your attention a couple of techniques that will help your investing longevity and success. Life has a way of shaking us up, presenting challenges, and we cannot let our mistakes and disappointments prevent us from reaching for our dreams. I learned if I am not making mistakes I am not taking risks and barely living. The investing world is often a lonely place because a very small percentage of the population has the stick with it attitude, and follow through to be an investor. I am not a Psychologist but it seems people often want to bring you down to their deflated and victim mentality. Be strong, my friends, and reach for your dream to be real estate rich! Write down what you want, no matter how crazy or out of reach it may seem to you now. Go ahead, just write it down on paper and put it in a drawer. You will find your dreams and desires become more real when you put them on paper. When your motivation is wavering, you may not be looking and miss out on a great deal. You are hearing about this person and that person who has made some crazy money from real estate deals, but you still seem to be pushing your canoe through the weeds. Go to your list of desires and dreams, and know that persistence is the magic of any successful person. If this were easy everyone would be doing it, right? Many, many successful people paid their dues, put in time, fell down, got back up, and kept moving forward. You hear about successful people only after they have kicked around in the dirt and paid their dues, to achieve success. If you are not making any mistakes, then you are not taking action. To take action inherently involves some risk. Life is like that; no risk, no reward. Do not fear making a mistake, this is your learning ground. No one—absolutely no one—who has accumulated a real estate portfolio, began investing knowing everything, making all the right choices, or immediately making buckets of money.

Stay the course and remind yourself why you wanted to buy real estate. Your reasons for buying real estate are personal for you. My motivation to accumulate real estate is different from your motivation. The thing that is important to remember if and when Mr. Impatient comes to visit in your mind, remember that real estate appreciates over time and, eventually, you own that house or rental condo free and clear. You can achieve when you believe. There have always been, and always will be, naysayers who believe real estate is going to crash, or the bubble is going to burst any moment. I personally know of people who have been complaining about real estate prices while they continue play video games. What action are they taking to add some security to their financial future? Granted that is a generalization about a segment of the population but, generally, I have seen this to be true. Consider who is telling you information about the state of the market or the economic stability of the country for that matter, often it's the armchair critic.

Real estate does not increase value in a straight line. Neither is your overall success going to play out in a straight line. So, when you fall down and scrape your knees, get up, brush yourself off, and get back in the game! Virtually everyone you will talk with wishes they could invest in real estate. You are doing it! Pat yourself on the back, give yourself a break, take vacations, and continue moving forward.

Take Care of Your Health

The most important element to investing success is you! You have been given one physical body, no exchanges, no returns. Although modern science is advancing rapidly with organ replacement and cell development, it would still be prudent to take care of what you have. You have a bright future ahead of you with a secure nest egg of equity building in real estate. You want to travel to live a long, healthy, and happy life. Poor health is a drag and prematurely depletes your energy and enthusiasm. Preserve the temple, your body; it will transport you around while operating at peak performance. You are going to have a comfortable lifestyle in later years, so you want to enjoy that time, right? If you are a hands-on renovation guy or gal, go easy on those knees when installing flooring and take care of your back lifting toilets and huge pieces of drywall. Let the younger ones carry the drywall or tiles into the house. You do not need to be a hero or prove anything to anyone by abusing or pushing past your physical limitations.

Investing in real estate, depending on the risk level, can take a toll on your health. Financial stress will wear you down mentally, and physically. There is a positive motivating stress or mild fear, but that is not what I am talking about here. Financial stress ruins marriages and is like a monkey on your back that goes everywhere with you. Invest within your means and carefully think through before entering into more risky investing situations. You will come across, or be presented, the *sure thing* that will require little work but return you buckets of cash. Beware of the big talkers with unrealistic promises. When you invest always have a plan B. Preserve your home life and family security when making investing decisions. Your home and your family come before buying one more investment property. You would never want to jeopardize your family home for a risky investment deal gone bad.

Stress can be difficult to detect but it is patient and will work you over through lack of sleep, poor digestion, over eating, and more advanced results of stress are difficulty in making sound decisions leading to family break ups, company failure, isolation and depression. When your nervous system is on high alert for a long period of time due to, say, being highly financially leveraged for a long period of time, your internal organs cease operating properly. Doctors call this your fight or flight response. Financial stress triggers this response in your body and your body is constantly on alert. Over time your body cannot sustain such response and begins to get sick. Your body is a remarkable machine and will keep going for you when it is sick. It will adapt the best it can to keep operating as you push through stressor after stressor. Then, one day, you are diagnosed with some traumatic disease. You ask yourself how did this happen? Did you treat your body well? Did you feed it nutritious foods? Did you give it the rest it needed? Did you take vacations? Did you hydrate (due to the fact that the majority of our body is composed of water)?

I was long winded about stress because we seem to be getting busier and busier with life. Be cautious and enjoy.

Treat your body and mind well, and it will carry you in good health later on down the road.

Enjoy Life

Life is short. Don't be too critical of yourself and accept that you will make mistakes. Enjoy your family, enjoy the process of buying and watching your real estate investment grow.

I hope you have received some knowledge to take away to further your investing. I have attempted to share my passion for real estate with you in this brief how-to book.

Enjoy what you have and not what you do not have. If you read this book, chances are very good you can achieve the success you desire. The reasons for buying real estate are *yours*—not your brother's or your best buddy's—yours and *only* yours. Whatever your vehicle for accumulating wealth put the pedal to the metal. If you invest in something other than real estate, thoroughly investigate the opportunity, and I wish you all the success. Besides, everyone cannot be real estate investors—the playing field would be too crowded. Be confident with what you dream for, and go for it! Work hard and reward yourself, however that looks for you. Real estate markets will fluctuate, relationships will come and go, babies will be born, jobs will be won and lost, but one thing is certain—no one can ever take your dreams from you! So, get out there, scuff up your knees, kick around in the dirt and be the best *you* that you can be!

Notes

Notes

About the Author

Doug McIntyre lives in Vancouver, Canada, and is currently an investor and real estate agent.

The author is available to take on clients looking to buy or sell their home or purchase local real estate for investment.

The author is available for delivering keynote presentations to small or large groups. For rates and availability, contact the author directly at You2CanOwnRealEstate.com.

To order more books, contact amazon.com.

Finally, if you are inspired by this book, pass it on to another, or direct your friends, family, and coworkers to Doug's website at: You2CanOwn RealEstate.com. We all love to talk about real estate, but so many sit on the sidelines with lack of knowledge and know-how to make that first-time purchase, investment, or joint venture deal.

For Bonuses go to
www.you2canownrealestate.com

- Insider not widely known tips and tricks
- Download the most recent residential average home prices in your area
- Graph showing the rise of real estate over time
- Up to date $/sq. ft. renovation costs
- Information about real estate trends and general articles of interest
- Notice of local real estate events